The Logic
of Enlightenment

A Cognitive Theory of Spirituality

The Logic
of Enlightenment

A Cognitive Theory of Spirituality

Dave S. Henley

BOOKS

Winchester, UK
Washington, USA

First published by iff Books, 2015
iff Books is an imprint of John Hunt Publishing Ltd., Laurel House, Station Approach,
Alresford, Hants, SO24 9JH, UK
office1@jhpbooks.net
www.johnhuntpublishing.com
www.iff-books.com

For distributor details and how to order please visit the 'Ordering' section on our website.

Text copyright: Dave S. Henley 2014
Library of Congress Control Number: 2015934342

ISBN: 978 1 78535 038 2

A CIP catalogue record for this book is available from the British Library.

Design: Stuart Davies

Printed and bound by CPI Group (UK) Ltd, Croydon, CR0 4YY, UK

We operate a distinctive and ethical publishing philosophy in all
areas of our business, from our global network of authors to
production and worldwide distribution.

CONTENTS

TO THE MEMORY OF

Alida Erasmus and Richard Clarke

Neither the logical or theoretical mode of search – the ancient organon – nor the experimental modern mode, or organon – has answered in a direct manner. So that it seems there must be some lack in the reasoning processes yet invented…

… Now the endeavour to make discoveries is like gazing at the sky up through an oak tree. Here a beautiful star shines through between the boughs: here a constellation is hidden by a branch: a universe by a leaf. Some mental or logical organon is required enabling us to distinguish… when the apparently immovable obstacle is only a leaf…

… Some day a puff of wind will push the leaf aside, and the marvel will then be that the object was not observed long since.

Richard Jefferies, The Story of My Heart (1st draft)

Introduction

Spirituality is widely recognized as a significant experience in life; however, it is poorly understood and indeed barely acknowledged at all by rationalists. The aim of this work is to provide a definitive rational account of spiritual enlightenment that does justice both to reason on the one hand, and to spirituality on the other.

Many people feel a need for spiritual enlightenment because of a requirement for some deeper meaning, or perhaps because of a pervading sense of emptiness and futility, in life. For, despite the apparent reasonableness of all our practical aims, we may nevertheless suffer a continuing malaise, or even depression, that no rational improvement in our circumstances seems able to alleviate, and which only such a non-rational change as enlightenment can apparently cure. Why should this be? One reason may be that we sometimes feel our inmost being is in conflict, not with any particular situation in which we find ourself, and which might therefore be improved, *but with life as a whole*. But what then is life as a whole, and what is our inmost being? It is notable in this regard that the world's major religions have all identified a higher human nature or sense of self (soul) from which we can become dislocated or dissociated. This dissociation, which goes under various names e.g. sin in Christianity and suffering in Buddhism, is said by them to be what causes us to lose our way in life.

Yet, while they may still feel a need to be enlightened spiritually, many people may not feel able to commit themselves to any associated religious or spiritual beliefs. Enlightenment of the kind found in Buddhism, however, requires no such belief, but only some experience of a 'higher' identity or self-awareness, in addition to the thinking, feeling self with which we are all familiar. This experience, for want of a better word, we may call our sense of spiritual identity. Such a spiritual sense of self does not commit us to the existence of spirit or of a soul, or indeed any spiritual belief whatsoever, but merely delimits a sphere of interest; and of the existence of this sphere of interest there can be little doubt. At the same time, this also admits the possibility of a philosophical work that might provide a fully secular account of enlightenment. Such an account is developed here, in which the reader is required to believe nothing that is not logically demonstrated in the text, step by step from her own familiar experiences. It provides a definitive explanation of the fact, noted by each religion, that our desolation can sometimes be conquered by means of a special life-changing experience variously called 'redemption' or 'salvation', as well as 'enlightenment', which makes life intelligible, and even blissful. As part of the investigation, the logical and psychological status of enlightenment, together with its practical benefits, are carefully identified and analysed.

We may not ordinarily notice the spiritual identity that enlightenment reveals to us, but we certainly notice its absence. Just as we only tend to notice the air that we breathe when it is in short supply, so we also tend to notice our higher sense of self when we feel it is being stifled. This occurs when we experience a clash between being true to ourself, on the one hand, and acting according to how we perceive the demands of the world around us on the other. The effect then is that the world becomes strange to us, we understand life only with difficulty, it no longer comes naturally to us. It is foreign to our nature. We become alienated. Such alienation is not directed at anything in particular, and the corresponding enlightenment that liberates us from it is, therefore, not specific either. By contrast, if for instance a man feels depressed at losing his job, then simply finding another job may make him feel better. Or, even if he feels lonely and rejected, then finding a group that finally accepts him as he is might suffice to make him happy for perhaps the first time.

Fundamental as these deprivations may be, they are still relatively specific; but I am speaking of something even more general, of what is sometimes called an existential crisis, for which no rational cure exists.

However, contrary to the existentialist view that alienation is a realistic or even inevitable response to the human condition, we here investigate philosophically the process of spiritual enlightenment, in which we may either suddenly or more gradually be said to acquire a spiritual sense of whom we really are and what life is all about. The consequent contrast with existentialism here is tantamount to urging a quite different view of the human condition. To illustrate this difference consider the words of an American mystic, Thoreau, in a cabin in the woods 'in the midst of a gentle rain':

> I was suddenly sensible of such sweet and beneficent society in Nature, in the very pattering of the drops, and in every sight and sound around my house, an infinite and unaccountable friendliness all at once, like an atmosphere, sustaining me, as made the fancied advantages of human neighbourhood insignificant, and I have never thought of them since. Every little pine-needle expanded and swelled with sympathy and befriended me. I was so distinctly made aware of the presence of something kindred to me, that I thought no place could ever be strange to me again.
>
> Henry David Thoreau, *Walden*

Far from being in conflict with the world as a whole, Thoreau experienced the exact opposite: complete harmony with the world as a whole. This naturally prompts the question: how might a transition from one state to the other be possible? Only by a thoroughgoing transformation of all one's thought processes, by altering the entire way in which you use your own mind. This means nothing less than altering the way we engage with reality, that is changing our criteria of what we consider rational, and of when we consider ourself to understand or not understand something. As a result, what formerly seemed illogical may now come to seem logical and vice versa. In this way, we are put in touch with our deepest sense of who we are. Along with this we might also expect our standards of success and failure to change, e.g. instead of success depending only on outer results we may now be more concerned with inner fulfilment. Instead of measuring ourself by external yardsticks, our new 'spiritual' sense of self now allows us to judge instead the adequacy of each and every yardstick. Situations which were previously confused now resonate with meaning.

The effect of such enlightenment is a radical change from insecurity and estrangement in the world to security and familiarity, even though nothing about the world may have changed. And just as no good fortune can ever cheer the depressive, so no misfortune can now depress the enlightened mystic, largely because they are using their minds in these very different ways. Our task will be, therefore, to endeavour to explain these different ways of using one's mind and, thereby, explain the crucial concept of enlightenment. Yet how can we presume to do so if, as is claimed, a defining characteristic of 'enlightenment' is that it cannot be put into words?

The answer is that we do not aspire to do the impossible, which is to define enlightenment in words. Rather, we accept that it is indefinable, but instead we seek to explain why it *must* be indefinable. We accept its mystical nature, but we seek to explain *why* it must be mystical, and how it could not succeed in what it achieves unless it were mystical. The reason is because it alters the way we understand things and events in our life, and for it to *not* be mystical, enlightenment would have to already be understandable in terms of our current conceptions. In that case, it would not express such an extreme life change, and we might instead be able to cure our alienation by the use of reason or a change of circumstances. But this is precisely what seems to be impossible; rather, it is a change in our understanding itself, of who we are, that makes life magically appear to switch from the existentially meaningless to one of profound meaning. This investigation will make these matters much more precise and, paradoxically, we shall hope thereby to learn, by the very act of specifying in words exactly *why* enlightenment cannot be put into words, something about what enlightenment itself is. This is because a crucial part of enlightenment is an inner under-standing of the very difference between what is, and what is not, conceivable in thought. It is in this way that we endeavour to provide a satisfactory rational account of an experience that is, in itself, non-rational.

Our understanding of 'life as a whole' must, in order to be relevant to particular events, also bear upon the meaning of our particular thoughts, and hence upon the very nature of all human understanding in general. For if, due to enlightenment, our understanding of life alters, so the nature of our thoughts alters also, since the thought of the enlightened mystic is very different in nature from the thoughts of the depressive or the existentialist. In fact, it will be demonstrated that, in a precise sense, the latter tend to adhere to fixed concepts, while the mystic is more flexible, habitually allowing for new meaning. Indeed, the thesis is argued that what we call enlightenment is, at the same time, the fount and origin of all new meaning. It is concluded that there is, consequently, an irreducibly mystical component at the very heart of all human cognition, which currently goes unacknowledged by science. And it is our intimate acquaintance with this mystical component that consti-tutes our enlightenment. In other words, it becomes clear that the key to living life successfully turns out also to be the key to solving problems in general; the key to our higher intelligence.

For example, it will become clear how, and in what way, enlightenment can enable us to understand our own contra-dictory thoughts, and thereby engage with the many conflicts and dilemmas which blight our lives. This is 'The Middle Way' of Buddhism. Grasping contradictions must necessarily be mystical, as it goes beyond the limits of our concepts. It cannot be accomplished by conceptual thought – since the very moment a thought contradicts itself it ceases to be a thought. And, since it comprehends these contradictions, enlightenment itself cannot, therefore, be comprehensible in thought. Thus, while enigmatic or contradictory utterances have been central to many mystical and religious traditions, such as Sufism and Zen, it is shown here how such a mystical understanding can actually have rational and cognitive value also.

In this way, by studying the nature of meaning, we discover something important about what it is to be human. Indeed, we discover that the real nature of Man is to be a maker of new meaning and, contrary to Descartes, is not merely to be a thinker, a user of current meanings. It is thus seen how spiritual enlightenment is capable of assisting our most ordinary beliefs and choices, and of thereby illuminating life as it is actually lived and experienced. Because our life is guided, and indeed directed, by individual thoughts and concepts, so it is shown that to alter the limits of these thoughts and concepts via enlightenment must also be to alter by non-rational means the limits of our life. Moreover, like the early Wittgenstein, it is being suggested that the nature of these limits can only be fully comprehended by a logical engagement with the mystical. The result is a new understanding of who we are, and how to act in life.

If our original malaise was all along due to life not making sense, that is to failing to understand life, then it may not, after all, come as a surprise if both the loss and the renewal of meaning in life should be linked to a mystical component at the very centre of how we grasp and create meaning in general. If so, then comprehending the nature and function of this mystical component is enlightenment. We commence our investigation though with the very opposite of enlightenment, that is with such a sense of emptiness and futility in our thinking and reasoning that we may entirely lose our direction, or our sense of self, or both.

Chapter 1

The Problem of Life

The cartoon (Fig. 1)[1] can be interpreted superficially as a tramp asking a complete stranger information about his own name and his own intentions, and the inappropriateness of such a question is fairly amusing at this level. Of course, it is even possible that the desk clerk knows this tramp, and so does actually know the answers to his questions, when interpreted this way.

But at a deeper level, the tramp's identity is not in any case given by his name, nor his destination by a particular place, thus making it impossible for the desk clerk to answer him. Rather, this tramp now symbolizes everyman, and his impoverished state surely depicts the poverty of his understanding of himself.

His question inquires as to his real identity and his true purpose in life, and the further question raised is not: can this be answered by information from a stranger, but: is it the kind of question that can be answered by information at all? The humour now lies in the absurdity of suggesting that mere factual information is capable of answering life's deepest questions. Self-knowledge certainly seems to be knowledge of some kind, and yet perhaps not knowledge of information. But if not information, what other kind of knowledge is there? It is this that we shall investigate.

As an example of feeling this loss of identity in real life consider the following:

> I open my eyes and don't know where I am or who I am. Not all that unusual – I've spent half my life not knowing. Still, this feels different. This confusion is more frightening. More total...
>
> ... Consequently my mind doesn't feel like my mind. Upon opening my eyes I'm a stranger to myself, and while, again, this isn't new, in the mornings it is more pronounced. I run quickly through the basic facts. My name is Andre Agassi... I play tennis for a living, even though I hate tennis, hate it with a dark and secret passion, and always have.
>
> Andre Agassi, *Open*

I should call this: losing one's sense of oneself *spiritually*; in one way Agassi knows perfectly well who he is, he is the author of his thoughts and actions, and the subject of all his feelings. But it is in a spiritual sense, the sense of knowing how to act in a way that is truly meaningful and fulfilling to him, that he has lost track. This is a distressing state of mind, and when we are in this state no instruction is more perplexing than 'Just be yourself', for one does not know where to begin. Being ourself is the one role we cannot be taught, precisely because it is not a role as such but is rather the way we approach every role, and no one can tell us how to do that. Neither can this spiritual sense of self even be regarded as somehow the aggregate of all the roles I take in my various relationships, since one can experience this desolation at the same time as conducting any or all of these relationships.

Such a state can generate a morbid depression leading even to thoughts of suicide, as the author Leo Tolstoy attested. 'At about the age of fifty,' writes William James,[2] 'Tolstoy relates that he began to have moments of perplexity, of what he calls arrest, as if he knew "not how to live", or "what to do". "I felt," said Tolstoy, "that something had broken within me on which my life had always rested, that I had nothing left to hold on to, and that morally my life had stopped. An invincible force impelled me to get rid of my existence, in one way or another."' Tolstoy survived his despair, but Van Gogh's ominous painting *Wheatfield with Crows* exhibits the same directionless quality, by depicting a path which peters out, together with crows as harbingers of death. It was painted shortly before the artist took his own life.

False identity

Existentialist philosophers have referred to this loss of identity as *alienation*: an extremely painful, even unbearable, state. To escape this emptiness of existence the mind often then seems to compensate by manufacturing an idealized artificial self to give meaning to our actions, and to make life bearable. The lack of a sense of self may now be filled by a set of thoughts and images which we adopt as ideal criteria for how we ought to think and act. If, for example, we only pride ourself on whenever we succeed in attaining these criteria, then this is an unmistakeable sign that we have developed an ego. If, however, we fail to live up to the ideal requirements of this self-image relentlessly 'pressing down' on us, the result may be depression and feelings of inferiority or failure. The feelings of ego and failure may seem to be very different; nevertheless the reality is that in both cases we experience a similar sense of low self-esteem. This is surely because in both cases we have become the mere puppet of a self-image that is foreign to, yet esteemed above, whom we naturally are. A teenage girl may be dominated by her image in the mirror, Agassi had to win every match, and even Tolstoy reported his compulsion to perfect himself physically, mentally and morally.

Jean-Paul Sartre employed the notion of a self-image to make a fundamental claim about human nature, namely that the only way for man to be free is to lack any such conception of his own identity. In a famous example he described a man self-consciously acting out the role of a waiter, having the idea of a perfect waiter in his head. Sartre calls this 'bad faith' because the waiter so completely identifies with his role that he believes his options to be determined only by this idea. In this way he curtails all the other choices that exist for him as a human being which in reality are restricted only by the power of his imagination. Thus any self-image misrepresents the true nature of human freedom. To live what Sartre calls an 'authentic', and therefore free, life is to acknowledge the choices that really exist for you, without hiding behind artificial restrictions that can be used as excuses.

It follows that the choices available to man thus cannot be defined by any single idea or concept, however complex. In this respect man differs from an artefact, which Sartre says – using the example[3] of a paper knife – is 'producible in a certain manner and one which, on the other hand, serves a definite purpose.' Thus the artefact may be said to have a particular *essence*. Furthermore, he adds that 'there is at least one being whose existence comes before its essence, a being which exists before it can be defined by any conception of it. That being is man.' Thus for man, *existence precedes essence*. Sartre called this view Existentialism.

Man cannot be defined by any one particular essence or concept of himself precisely because he can grasp all possible concepts, any of which can be used by him to guide his actions.

The only fact about himself invariably given to the mind of man is that he exists, and his nature or essence therefore can only be whatever he creates for himself. While the flexibility of this view might seem to liberate man from stereotypes, what then is the purpose of man? For Sartre, man has no innate purpose; his only purposes are those of his own devising. Furthermore, if there is no ultimate conception of man or his destiny for us to hold on to, then we appear to be adrift in an endless sea of possibilities, with no guidance as to how to act. Like the tramp in the cartoon, man has become directionless and lost his identity; Sartre called this the Human Condition. However, it will be my aim to demonstrate that Sartre was mistaken, and that it is indeed possible to find a conception of ourself by which to comprehend our innermost identity.

Every 'identity' we make we can, in principle, unmake. Even our closest relationships: husband, father, lawyer, friend do not compel my actions, are not what make them *my* actions, for I am always free to act in any other way I can imagine, and still be me. I may indeed be compelled to act in certain ways by my relationships but, says Sartre, it is I who choose those relationships. The true nature of human freedom is that whatever identity I adopt can always be reappraised; and because this is always hard work we arrive at Sartre's paradoxical conclusion that (psychological) freedom is a burden. Here, it is not acting responsibly that is identified as the burden, but the choosing of where my responsibility lies, for Sartre says that 'there exists a specific consciousness of freedom' and that this consciousness is always one of *anguish*. Anguish or existential angst is another one of Sartre's terms and is intended to be as devoid of material content, as freedom itself is. The 'anguish' of such freedom resides in our being unable to find any basis for choosing one action over another that can ever be regarded as ultimate or intrinsic to our nature. If we base the action upon any moral or political code, any religious doctrine or idea of ourself, these are all values or systems of belief that we ourself freely choose. With bitter irony, Sartre declares: we are 'condemned to be free' for no relationship or idea we hold about ourself is ultimately justified in telling us how to act: we are condemned to confusion and indecision. It would be a different matter if we were made in the image of God: then divine guidance might tell us how to act. However, in this work we accept the problem in the same terms as Sartre, namely: as one that needs to be addressed in secular language without assuming any supernatural entities.

We now seem to reach the absurd conclusion that it is the alienated individual, the least committed to roles and relationships, who is the most free i.e. the most true to the human condition in which we all find ourselves. In other words it is the tramp in the cartoon who did not know who he was nor where he was going, or Tolstoy who was so directionless he knew not how to live, that now appear to be our role models of freedom. Sartre calls this existing authentically despite lacking an ultimate essence, but we can surely call it existing without really *living*, existing without really experiencing life, living only half a life. For surely, if my only identity is merely to exist, then paradoxically the most authentic person would be one who is unencumbered by any other sense of self that might appear to give his life an illusory direction or purpose. A person who, in other words, by lacking these very assets, is consequently not fully living! It seems we are victims of a cruel dilemma: if we are truly free, then life has no purpose; if we give purpose to our life, then we are not truly free. Indeed, in the existentialist works of Kafka, Beckett, Camus, and Sartre himself, the protagonists are often just such alienated and confused individuals.

Surely, however, there must be something wrong with such a conception of freedom, in which the most free individuals are those who are unable to act at all, either from confusion or because they are paralyzed with indecision? In effect, such persons are only proposed as being the most true to themselves, because it is believed there really is no self to be true to.

Spiritual freedom

In fact, Sartre's concept of freedom is almost a parody of ordinary speech, where in practice freedom is ordinarily viewed as an attractive thing and which, far from being a burden, represents the shedding of all burdens as a form of release and liberation. When we say we yearn to be free, do we really mean we are yearning for a burden? Rather, the complete opposite. This common usage of 'free' actually agrees far more closely with Eastern spirituality than with existentialism. We might more plausibly say, therefore, that the common usage means being spiritually free in some sense, rather than existentially free. Spiritual freedom means that, far from free choices being 'hard work' and agonizing, they are now effortless and even exhilarating. And far from living only half a life, the free individual now feels fully alive. Somehow choices now feel natural to us, indicating that they do in some sense express our real nature. Of course, executing the chosen action may well be hard work and painful, but the prior act of choice, the freedom itself, is now effortless and painless. This must be because, in some sense, truly knowing who I am (and hence knowing what I want) must also be effortless, contrary to Sartre's view that ultimately there is no me to be known.

Now, since both these opposing kinds of freedom are claimed to be the ultimate arbiter in deciding how to act, they are consequently in genuine conflict. In order to resolve this contradiction it will be necessary to investigate the concept of freedom found in Eastern spirituality. But firstly, a Western allegory may help. The two conscious experiences of freedom are distinctively different mental states, and I believe the biblical metaphor of Exodus, historically celebrated in Judaism during Passover, may also be said, on a psychological interpretation, to symbolize both these two mental states. Here, the bondage of the Israelites in Egypt could stand for the 'bad faith' of identifying internally with an image of oneself, or with a particular social role or belief, for maintaining any such identity is hard work in a 'foreign land'. The Promised Land 'flowing with milk and honey' would then by contrast stand for spiritual freedom. I shall also eventually argue that the confusing 'freedom' of Sartre is represented by wandering lost in Sinai, resulting finally in a transition from the anguish of both existential freedom and bad faith, to the joy of spiritual freedom. In this way the Exodus, along with many other religious myths and legends, can be seen as symbolizing a very real psychological process that can be life-changing.

What is expressed in the West only by such religious allegories seems to find more explicit expression in the Eastern philosophical tradition as a concept of spiritual freedom. This Eastern concept of freedom is very different from our modern existential concept, and ultimately rests on a fundamentally different view of the human condition. To explore this idea of spiritual freedom, we begin with a recent radical thinker from the Indian tradition, J. Krishnamurti. In a series of almost Socratic dialogues, Krishnamurti repeatedly confronted Western attitudes and lifestyles with the challenge of Eastern wisdom. In one such dialogue the questioner expresses a Sartre-like disapproval of his own social conformity and asks how he can become free of conformity. Krishnamurti replies:

> One conforms instinctively for various reasons: out of attachment, fear, the desire for reward, and so on. That is one's first response. Then somebody comes along and says that one must be free from conditioning, and there arises the urge not to conform. Do you follow?
> J. Krishnamurti, *Commentaries on Living*, 3rd Series

The 'somebody' here could almost be Sartre himself, advocating the 'authentic' life. But now Krishnamurti says something surprising: he points out that the urge not to conform is not substantially different from the urge to conform, for he says:

> Surely, not to put an end completely to the mechanism that produces patterns, moulds, whether positive or negative is to continue in a modified pattern or conditioning.

By a mould or pattern Krishnamurti here means any fixed concept or idea by which the mind guides all its preferences and decides all its actions. If we apply the above observation to Sartre's criticism of bad faith, we notice that not only is the self-image or ego of the waiter such a fixed concept (mould) to which the waiter conforms, but also Sartre's own idea of the *authentic individual* by which it is to be replaced is such a fixed concept. I.e. Sartre's whole theory of there being no concept or essence of a self adequate to guide our preferences is nevertheless a concept or essence by means of which we are being urged to guide our preferences instead. And to act 'authentically' is to choose to *conform* to this concept. This is because, here, deliberately not conforming to any (direct) idea of the self is nevertheless still conforming to an idea *intended to decide our actions*. Moreover, since this latter idea concerns nothing more than choosing between our own internal thoughts, it surely must also be (indirectly) an idea of the self. In other words, it seems that Sartre has just replaced one idea of the self with another. For an idea of oneself as merely existing without an essence, but for whom all choices therefore remain possible, seems still to be a fixed, if unpalatable, idea of oneself.

Krishnamurti, however, is saying that in order to truly free the mind, to achieve spiritual freedom, it must be entirely released from the 'mechanism' or thought process of creating new 'moulds' or concepts of itself so that, whenever one concept of the self is rejected, it is not merely replaced by another such concept, albeit more abstract. What Krishnamurti is asking us to do is to 'put an end', not to this or that fixed concept of oneself, but to *all* concepts of self however abstract, and the thought process that produces them. But how is this 'putting an end' to the thought process of defining ourselves to be accomplished? Krishnamurti appears to imply that one can simply refrain from thinking about one's own nature. This indeed is what he affirms at other places, where he seems also to endorse the process of meditation, whether formal or informal, as a means of achieving this. For, in nearly all forms of Eastern meditation, as a prelude to deeper mental states, a first step has been to eliminate all thought.

In order to do justice to the issue raised by Sartre and Krishnamurti, it will evidently be advantageous to examine the origins of each view within their respective traditions. This will entail investigation of the philosophy of Rene Descartes on the one hand, and of Hinduism and Buddhism on the other. As this work proceeds, the reader will therefore find that we shall, as here, alternate freely between Eastern thought and Western thought.

Chapter 2

Mystical Experience

Tolstoy's Redemption

Tolstoy eventually rediscovered his reason to live but, gifted author though he was, it was not a reason he was able fully to put into words, and so serves to illustrate well the enigmatic nature of Redemption or Enlightenment. Indeed, he believed it was his very ability to reason in words that had led him astray and let him down, as he expresses eloquently via a character, Levin, in *Anna Karenina:*

> … he had been stricken with horror, not so much of death, as of life… The physical organization, its decay, the indestructibility of matter, the law of conservation of energy, evolution, were the *words* which usurped the place of his old belief. These words and the ideas associated with them were very well for intellectual purposes. But for life they yielded nothing, and Levin felt suddenly like a man who has changed his warm cloak for a muslin garment, and going for the first time into the frost is immediately convinced, *not by reason, but by his whole nature* that he is as good as naked, and that he must infallibly perish miserably. [My italics]

Tolstoy seems to be saying it is as much the experience of his body as of his mind that creates Levin's instinctive reaction to the chill of the intellect. This metaphor of clothing is relevant also to the tramp in Fig. 1, whose ragged coat also implies he too lacks the necessary protection to make his way in the world. The humour here highlights the irony noted grimly by Tolstoy: that no amount of theoretical information can answer the vital question of life. We can now perhaps read the cartoon as saying that no theoretical *idea* of self (including even Sartre's idea of freedom) can liberate, since it cannot allow for acting instinctively. By acting instinctively, we mean acting not only according to our physical (lower) nature, but perhaps also according to the higher nature I have postulated. Tolstoy uses the above metaphor of a physical need (warmth) of our lower nature to symbolize a spiritual need of our higher nature. But whenever we act naturally, I shall argue that it may be either our lower nature or our higher nature that we are expressing.

Clearly, the cartoon may now be regarded as depicting the complete person, with both the clerk and the tramp as parts of the same mind. Interpreted thus, it now suggests that there is no idea the conscious mind (the clerk) can provide that can tell the whole person (including the tramp) how to act instinctively, in either a higher or a lower sense. This means no ideas can tell us how to be ourself. Indeed as Tolstoy said, it seems these ideas actually *prevent* us being ourself. If the man at the desk dominates our life, then we turn our real self into a tramp; we become spiritually homeless.

By confining ourself only to ideas (even Sartre's) of ourself we impoverish our real sense of self. And yet Tolstoy describes how the complete person of Levin, uniting body and mind, is somehow able to instantly comprehend that he lacks something he needs, without knowing what. He feels that the new chill of intellect runs counter to his very nature. Samuel Beckett also often used the poverty of tramps to portray the human condition. In *Waiting for Godot*, Beckett similarly employs ill-fitting boots to signify the spiritual poverty of man despite all his knowledge, and has Vladimir saying, 'There's man all over for you. Blaming on his boots the faults of his feet.' Here, clothing is again being used to signify that although we can grasp some of life via our ideas, it is only with great discomfort that we do so, and that thought and reason are not fully adequate to our requirements, since they do not come *naturally* to us.

It is clear, however, that we have no conceptual description of what kind of behaviour constitutes acting naturally in the higher sense. For example, there can be no specific instructions telling a person how they are to act if they are to act naturally in this sense. There is no intended state of affairs that we need to bring about to achieve this result, and calculated efforts succeed only in preventing it, *since acting by calculation tends to be what we mean by acting unnaturally.* To act naturally is to be yourself, but thinking about yourself is clearly different from simply *being* yourself, either physically or spiritually. And so it is not natural, but self-conscious, to think about how you are acting, or how you ought to be acting. However, now it seems that, apart from our physical or biological nature, we have also found another nature, which we can call spiritual. Although we cannot characterize this nature literally, Tolstoy, Beckett and others have found aspects of our physical nature to provide useful metaphors for our spiritual nature. And it seems that we can act naturally either by appeasing our physical (lower) nature (e.g. physical appetites), but equally by appeasing our spiritual (higher) nature.

What kind of behaviour does in fact appease our higher nature? This should become clearer later, but for the moment we may notice that for each person it seems likely there is some sphere of activity that *comes naturally* to them. In these cases we have some knack or gift, which we are able to perform without calculation. Examples of this for suitably talented people can be: electronic design, dancing, mending cars, cookery and mathematics; for all these can contain an element of intuition in which decisions can be made freely (e.g. gestures in a dance) with the impression of not following any rule. Thus our higher nature seems to be an aspect of human cognition not involving thought.

Indeed, it was by some such realization that Tolstoy regained his faith in life. By observing how the serfs on his own estate appeared to ignore the dictates of Reason, he remarks in his *Confession*:

Yet how believe as the common people believe, steeped as they are in the grossest superstition? It is impossible – but yet their life! Their life! It is normal. It is happy! It is an answer to the question!

And indeed he makes his character Levin experience something of this answer, by actually taking on the work of one of his peasants:

> The longer Levin mowed, the oftener he felt the moments of uncon-sciousness in which it seemed not his hands that swung the scythe, but the scythe mowing of itself, a body full of life and consciousness of its own, and as though by magic, without thinking of it, the work turned out regular and well-finished of itself. These were the most blissful moments.

Here Levin was no longer confined to intellectual words but had found a new physical mode of understanding. Just as he was acting naturally in avoiding the cold, so he is now acting naturally in another, cognitive, sense: by seeming to avoid rational thought and calculation.

In real life Tolstoy, like Levin, was able to find his own reason to live, by apparently abandoning part of his own dependency on rational thought. His reasons are obscure, but William James quotes him as saying that he had mistakenly been:

> … looking for the value of one finite term in that of another, and the whole result could only be one of those indeterminate equations in mathematics which end with $0 = 0$.

> … but that, after enlightenment, he learnt to 'believe in the infinite as common people do'. It seems that by 'finite', Tolstoy meant conceivable in rational thought, and by 'infinite' he meant not conceivable in thought. Surely, taking such a fateful step is what is usually called, a leap of faith.

However, here we hope to do something rather better: to explain rationally how and why such a thing is possible and to justify such a move logically. Nevertheless, it is clear Tolstoy achieved spiritual redemption from his travails and, we may say, attained Enlightenment, despite the lack of such a logical analysis. Typically, those who have attained insight beyond thought can't *say* what they have learnt. But we will find a way. For what Tolstoy came to grasp seems to have been neither the unreason of the superstitions exhibited by his serfs, nor Levin's impeccable reasoning about the conservation of energy or evolution. In other words, his insight seems to have consisted neither of false theories, nor of true theories. In fact, it seems that what he came wordlessly to understand did not consist of theories at all. We shall see that the vital insight is actually a different mode of using your entire mind, and that it is this that, at the same time, provides a way of learning how to really be yourself.

As a first step on the road to a logical account of Enlightenment and spiritual self-knowledge, it will help to first analyse how we ordinarily use the word 'self'.

'Self' is used in two opposing senses

Supposing you go to the rescue of a stranded motorist: then you are obeying something in you that enables you to identify with a complete stranger. We might say that you are acting on behalf of your higher self, at the expense of the needs and interests of your lower self. Thus, corresponding to the two levels of human nature, there also seem to be two different concepts of self. When being self-centred or self-conscious we are always thinking about what we ordinarily conceive to be ourself, i.e. the thoughts or feelings or the needs or appearance of the person situated in a particular human body. Notice that even when being selfless and avoiding self-interest, the self whose needs and wishes we are now disregarding is still the self based upon our body, and the needs being disregarded are the physical and emotional needs based only upon that body. Let us call this self the *lower* self.

However, there is another, more profound, use of 'self'. Surely whenever we speak, for instance, of 'finding yourself' we do not mean you find your body or anything based upon your body. Nor do we even mean finding any thoughts, sensations or emotions that we did not know we had; so this self is unlike e.g. the Freudian unconscious. It is a more abstract notion of self altogether that is being 'found', more akin to our identity, and which agrees with what used to be called the soul; however, as previously mentioned, no supernatural entities are being presupposed in this account. In similar fashion, to know yourself or to be yourself does not mean knowing or being just your body or just your feelings and thoughts, however obscure or hidden these latter may be. Rather, we appear to mean something different. There are no thoughts and feelings so deeply hidden that the exposure of them amounts to 'finding yourself' or even 'knowing yourself' in this sense. For what we are describing does not consist of thoughts and feelings at all. Rather, we mean finding something common to you and everyone else, something universal. To absorb yourself in, say, bread-making is precisely to lose consciousness of all these thoughts and feelings, however buried, so that, in the very process, you seem instead to find something else, your higher self or soul. And perhaps too, we get to really *know* ourself at such moments. This may be said to be a physical form of meditation, in which to lose consciousness of your lower self is to at the same time gain awareness of your higher self.

I suggest this too is the underlying sense of self meant in *self-esteem* and self-respect, as well as in finding or losing yourself and knowing or being yourself, rather than one based upon being esteemed or valued by other people in your various social or personal relationships. For, I shall argue that what is respected or known in self-respect or self-knowledge *is not based upon our body or its mind at all*, and not therefore upon any relationships participated in by the body or the mind, either. For surely, it is not any of my achievements I respect, when I respect myself, but my resolve, or my sense of integrity. Even if our self-esteem may in practice often depend upon being respected by those around us, this is *only if* it is our inner self, our integrity and inner judgement, we feel they respect, not simply the outer benefits it produced. By contrast, pride (admiring oneself) is the exact opposite of self-esteem, for here it is indeed some achievement of one's body or mind that is being valued. While one may well take pride in one's achievements, intellect, skills or status compared to others, nevertheless to respect oneself is to know or value something other than merely these various attributes of oneself, or the truth of various beliefs that one holds about oneself. It seems to be due to knowledge of what we may call our *higher* self, and it enables us to care about others regardless of our relationship to them. Focusing upon the lower self, however, tends to prevent this.

Could there be some universal way of conceiving my higher self, so that the reason for my concern for other people is because the self I respect and esteem in others is *the same* as the self I respect or esteem in me? This might explain why only by respecting myself can I bring myself to respect others also. And more strongly than this, perhaps only by loving myself do I acquire the capacity to love other people. On the other hand, we also know that self-seeking (gratifying your own body or mind) can, ironically, be detrimental to your soul or higher self by actually repressing its needs. As we have noted, 'self' is being used in the lower sense even in e.g. self-sacrifice or self-denial, since depriving your body or mind may sometimes nevertheless fulfil or satisfy your higher self – which cannot therefore be the self being deprived.

In fact, our motive for acting selflessly and sacrificing our self-interest for the sake of others with whom we have no relationship is normally in order to serve the promptings of our higher self. In other words, the two selves appear to oppose each other: the gratification or fulfilment of one is often the denial of the other. Yet, confusingly, the same word 'self' is used for both. Nevertheless, in either case being yourself, whichever self it is, may always be said to be *acting naturally*. So one way to discern whether we are indeed acting on behalf of our higher nature is to firstly decide if we are acting naturally or by calculation, since to be true to either our higher or lower *nature* is by definition always to act naturally. Then having established this, we next need to decide which nature we were satisfying, since the two normally oppose each other. That is, we need to identify whether we were really motivated by a physical appetite or by some 'higher' prompting that we can call spiritual. Notice, however, that because of their very naturalness one nature can easily be used to symbolize the other; for example the higher nature was expressed *physically* by Tolstoy in two different ways: on the one hand by the metaphor of Levin seeking a warm cloak, and on the other hand by a physical activity – Levin scything the meadow.

When we help another person we often do so unthinkingly, i.e. naturally, as an act of our higher self, rather than as a result of thought and reason. Of course, in order for our help to be effective we do subsequently employ thought and reason, but it seems the initial impulse may best be described as some unthinking expression of a higher nature that we often fail to acknowledge.

Mysticism in action

Since Tolstoy's eventual insight was ultimately indescribable by him, but only expressible by images, we must be justified in referring to it as mystical. Yet we may feel we nevertheless do understand Levin's experience of scything the meadow and how it represented an understanding not expressible in words. It begins to seem as if there may be a way of understanding with our body what we cannot grasp in words or even thought.

Indeed whenever we acquire any knack or simple skill, we are hard put to say what it is we have just learnt. Even a master of literature like Tolstoy could describe the swinging of the scythe only metaphorically as 'moving of itself, a body full of life and consciousness of its own.'

In Japan the mystical nature of physical skill has long been recognized in various martial arts, and the following example about Zen Buddhism conveys more detail about the perfectibility of skill.

> The pupil cannot stop watching his opponent and his swordplay; he is always thinking how he can best come at him, waiting for the moment when he is off guard. In short, he relies all the time on his art and knowledge. By so doing he loses his presence of heart: the decisive thrust always comes too late and he is unable to 'turn his opponent's sword against him'… What is to be done? How does skill become 'spiritual' and how does sovereign control of technique turn into master swordplay? Only, so we are informed, by the pupil becoming *purposeless and egoless*. He must be taught to be detached not only from his opponent but from himself. [My italics]
> Eugen Herrigel, *Zen in the Art of Archery*

It seems that, unlike the pupil, the master swordsman has no picture in his mind; no conceptual thoughts mediate between his perception and action, and this makes it truly mystical. Every picture allows, by definition, for the possibility of alternative pictures, but the master swordsman has no pictures in his mind and so his actions are not conceived as having alternatives, but must be simply what they are. There can be no misleading picture causing him to fail, because there is no picture at all. The thought of failure, which is the origin of fear, has been removed and the fear extinguished.

How different this is from everyday life, in which failure is an ever-present possibility. This is because our actions no longer comprise pure physicality, but require, and cannot be conducted without, a great deal of conceptual thought. To every true thought there is always a corresponding false thought, its denial and choosing the wrong thought bring failure. But in the Zen case, the master swordsman is, we are told, in a mental state beyond thought, and hence beyond the true and the false. In this way, illusion and doubt have been eliminated; his actions are now spiritually free, but at the same time unwilled, because the will requires thoughts. Being egoless, moreover, means he has no thoughts about himself, and being purposeless means having no thoughts about what he is doing. But how then is he both self-aware and, at the same time, successful in his task? It is this that we shall investigate.

It is clear that there is a definite cognitive skill being exhibited by the master swordsman, but apart from this his ability is more than just a skill because it is *inventive*, i.e. when the pupil makes an artful stroke the master effortlessly outplays him. And I think we are asked to believe that this is not merely due to past experience, since if it were then it is possible that the pupil could devise a stroke the master had not seen before. However, the suggestion appears to be that this is impossible, rather that it is the master who intuitively plays the stroke which no amount of training or theoretical knowledge by the pupil could possibly anticipate. So, being inventive, the master's swordplay cannot merely be viewed as a learned reflex, or the repetition of years of practice. Rather, it is presented as expressing a bodily kind of intelligence that *goes beyond thought and reason*; exactly what Tolstoy wanted, and suggested through his character, Levin. What is new here though is that, in the passage quoted, Tolstoy did not suggest any inventiveness to Levin's mowing, just a simple rhythm. However, like Levin, the Zen master is acting naturally, his strokes result from his higher nature; perhaps this may in turn be said to confer a corresponding higher intelligence upon his actions.

Now consider the implication as regards methodology, of trying to define this kind of intelligence by psychological or behavioural experiment. Any psychometric test would seek to identify necessary and sufficient conditions defining the skill of the master – precisely the kind of thinking previously being attempted by the pupil in his swordplay. In other words, the criteria employed by any psychometric test could in principle also be implemented by a suitably calculating pupil and, if correct, could lead him to victory over the master. But, we are told, there is no possibility of the pupil being correct; hence that there is no possibility of any such psychometric test being correct. A corollary is that no computer or robot could be programmed to simulate master swordplay because, if so, then the pupil could program himself in the same way, and thereby defeat the master.

Thus if we accept Herrigel's account at face value, and the authenticity of the Zen experience, it would seem to follow that certain kinds of physical ability can never be fully characterized by psychometric means, but must forever be regarded as intuitive, or indefinable. If, for instance, instead of swordplay we considered the game of tennis, we do find that a similar Zen-like state can occur in which a player is said to be 'in the zone' wherein his anticipation is such that the ball may now look twice as big, and he seems to have so much time to play his strokes that he feels he is playing in slow motion. Our question later will be whether these observations can be extended from physical activities to purely mental activities also.

What is surprising is that these very human considerations appertain to such physical examples at all. E.g. the same Zen-like mastery may repose in the daily work of a car mechanic (or indeed in one of Tolstoy's peasants) who is somehow able to see a car engine as an organic whole, and seems to have the uncanny knack, merely from informally inspecting one or two components, to know the likely source of failure. Of course this may be due purely to past experience, but equally from the above considerations it may not; for it may be a fault she has never seen before. Others, lacking this intuition or higher intelligence, and confined purely to reasoning from formal observation according to their theoretical knowledge, or to manufacturers' diagnostic charts, may be unable to correctly locate an unusual fault. Perhaps we might infer from this that mechanical aptitude and many other aptitudes may not, contrary to popular assumption, be adequately definable by psychometric tests, because every such test makes reference to some particular theory. And, if the Zen-like account is true, then no theory and hence no tests can stipulate for an intuition by somebody with a gift or aptitude the required outcome of that intuition.

There are countless other examples of intuition in action: the perfect timing of a political or business decision, which foils the opposition precisely because they are confined only to reasoning from past experience, and lack a current intuition of the situation as a whole.

Non-adversarial examples may include all cases of design, including: cookery, architecture, gardening, fashion, in which an intuition of the whole must guide each individual action. The manual dexterity of craftsmanship and even the shifting of furniture are all constantly inventive in small ways.

Finally, consider compassionate cases of human empathy. A teacher may be making slow but sure progress in teaching a deaf child to read, having painstakingly established a unique intuitive rapport with the child. Perhaps we might call this a kind of love. A new and inexperienced educational psychologist may now seek to evaluate the performance of both teacher and child via some form of psychometric monitoring. Seeing that the teacher is not conforming to the standard methods stipulated for a child of this age and attainment, the educational psychologist may then impose a teaching regimen foreign to the intuitive rapport that the teacher has with the child. The result of this insensitivity may be to frighten the child into mute submission, withdrawing all interest and active participation. One conclusion from an example such as this might be that love is not just a feeling, but can have a *cognitive* value, and provide a level of understanding that seems to go largely unrecognized by psychology. Clearly, this cognitive aspect of love, the ability to empathize, is personal and cannot be defined by any theory. Indeed, it was surely because the educational psychologist expressed only a theoretical interest in the child, not real love of the child, that she actually lacked the depth of understanding possessed by the teacher. And, since no psychometric test measures love, then no psychometric test can measure the particular aptitude for an activity (such as teaching) that love can bring to it. Ordinarily, we would not see anything mysterious in this; after all, people cannot be expected to be entirely rational. However, we have also seen that the same may be true of some of our relationships with machines and inanimate objects, and this does indeed seem to border on the mystical.

In this regard, I should now wish to argue that love in general, and not just personal relationships, intrinsically has a mystical aspect; this has long been claimed by poets, but we shall examine the matter somewhat more prosaically. For the moment, let us refer specifically to the love of some particular physical activity (like swordsmanship), and what circumstances make it possible. The first observation is that to love doing something is different from merely enjoying doing it or desiring to do it, since we may desire to do something for any number of reasons: to fulfil a lifelong ambition, to win admiration, to prove a point, or because it promotes a cause we believe in; and all of these may confer their own particular enjoyment. However, none of these may require me to *love* the activity itself, which requires first of all that the actual practice of the activity is desired and enjoyed for its own sake, and not merely as a means to some end. A boy may for instance dream of being a professional footballer or airline pilot, without having any idea of the hours of gruelling training, or the long periods of boredom that it may really entail. Real love of these activities implies *understanding* of their actual practice and not just liking the idea of them, just as real love of a person implies understanding of that person, and not just some idea of them.

Secondly, to love my work I must know that the work is fulfilling to me; this means not just that I enjoy it for its own sake, but that I am being *fully myself* in the performance of it, like Levin scything the grass. There should be some part of the task that comes *naturally* to me and that is not merely the careful application of reason to thoughts or observations like the Zen pupil, or the conscious following of rules. Actually, the 'part' of the task that comes to me naturally should be the 'egoless' sense of self that unites all the component activities into an organic whole, even if some of these component activities themselves consist only of analytical thoughts. It is this that provides the 'presence of heart' of the Zen swordsman, and the aptitude of the intuitive mechanic. Neither of these practitioners need necessarily love their work, but I am suggesting that, if they do, then they cannot do so without presence of heart. And this presence of heart is not any thought or feeling but is one's egoless sense of self which, according to Zen, excludes thought. From which it appears that this particular kind of love, the love of a physical or related activity, is not just a feeling but has a mystical component.

Furthermore, presence of heart in a physical activity seems to bring a success not obtainable without it. Thus love of an activity, as well as partaking of the mystical quality of acting naturally as a result of fully being oneself, also, as previously noted for empathy, seems to have a cognitive component. There is a Western literary conceit viewing the sensitive lover as being imbued with a special vulnerability, for example in *Death in Venice*, Thomas Mann associated love with decay, and in *The Idiot*, Dostoyevsky associated love with folly. However, here, on the contrary, the love of a physical activity is being identified as a sign of strength and prowess, in the form of a natural aptitude for that activity. As well as in Japanese Zen, this is also in keeping with the tradition of classical Greece, exemplified in its art; I am thinking in particular of two famous bronze statues: firstly the god Poseidon launching a javelin, and secondly the repose in action of a young charioteer at Delphi. Both exhibit a combination of serenity and mastery in which the love of the activity is clearly not just a feeling accompanying its performance regardless of results. Rather the love in some way *contributes to those results*, and is an indicator of ability in that activity that would not be measurable by psychometric tests. In short, to love an activity is to be good at it; although perhaps not conversely.

The nature of the mystical

We have seen that freedom, self and certain kinds of love may each be seen as possessing a mystical aspect. We now attempt to characterize the nature of mystical experience in general. Clearly one thing we mean by the mystical is an experience that cannot be defined or described in words. Of course, this would include the flavour of pineapple or the colour red and so we must also add that it is not observable by the senses, having no observable content. This aspect of the mystical is referred to as its ineffability. Poets have sometimes tried to convey this absolute unobservability by using the metaphor of observation by one sense in relation to unobservability by other senses. E.g. TS Eliot in the *Four Quartets* spoke of the 'deception of the thrush' suggesting that while we may hear the movements of a thrush over dead leaves in the shrubbery, we nevertheless cannot see it, but we know it is there. Similarly, the 'wild thyme unseen' is nevertheless smelled; both images symbolize the mystical conception that sense perception in general can sometimes *seem* to intimate to us the existence of something that is not available to sense perception at all.

As well as being ineffable and unobservable, a mystical experience is normally said to have a timeless quality, giving a subjective sense of time standing still. This was also symbolized by TS Eliot in the same work, using actual events in time:

> But only in time can the moment in the rose-garden,
> The moment in the arbour where the rain beat,
> The moment in the draughty church at smokefall,
> Be remembered; involved with past and future.
> Only through time time is conquered.

It is interesting to ask what kind of temporal episodes evoke a sense of being outside time in us; one possible answer is natural phenomena that are repetitive such as pattering raindrops or crashing waves or spiralling smoke, viewed from a place of stillness and safety such as an arbour or a church.

From another civilization, ancient China, another work: the *Tao Te Ching* of Lao Tzu also used concrete images to convey the content of mystical experience. He points out that the hub of a wheel contains empty space but that the use of a cart crucially depends on the use of this empty space. Similarly the use of a clay bowl depends upon the part of the bowl that is empty, i.e. not made of clay. Here Lao Tzu employs two kinds of physical existence in order to symbolize something not physically expressible at all, which he called the Tao. The physical material of the wheel or the bowl is being used to symbolize whatever is conceivable in thought, and the empty physical space of the hub or bowl expresses the mystical apprehension of something not conceivable in thought at all. He then uses this analogy to make the further point that what is beyond thought is both more useful and more important than what is thinkable. Of course this comparison cannot be made in thought, and so a poetic image has to be used: here two kinds of physical entity, matter and space, are being used to express what is within and what is beyond, the limits of thought. Wittgenstein did something similar with the logical syntax of language: the logical form of a sentence was said to symbolize what the sentence itself was unable to express.

Likewise, TS Eliot pointed out in the above verse that only in time can the timeless moment be remembered. Indeed we may add that only in time can the timeless moment be *experienced*, because only in time can anything at all be experienced (it only felt as if it was not in time). In these cases, temporal episodes somehow succeed in symbolizing for us a sense of not being temporal at all, i.e. of timelessness. And it is only by this symbolization, the last line seems to suggest, that we can comprehend timelessness at all and gain benefit from it. But by timelessness we conquer time, so paradoxically it is only by time itself that we conquer time. And one might equally say, in the case of the Tao, that it is only by concrete images, conceivable in thought, that the inconceivable Tao can be comprehended; so it is only by images of the conceivable itself that we are able to conquer the conceivable.

We can now attempt to summarize what we have learnt so far about the mystical. FC Happold[1] compiled a helpful list of the main characteristics of mystical states. These are:

- *Ineffability.* This means the state is not fully expressible in words, or conceivable in thought.
- They have a *noetic* quality, which means they seem to convey deep insights, and a new sense of understanding. The whole world becomes bathed in meaning.
- *Transiency.* Mystical experiences are normally of physically short duration, although they can seem timeless.
- *Passivity.* Mystical states seem to be something given to us and, while we can make ourself suitably receptive to them, they are not determined at all by our will.
- A sense of *oneness*. In a mystical experience the diverse

facts about the world seem to be united into a single organic whole. Out of the single Tao, for instance, the polar opposites of yin and yang are said to have sprung, creating the whole universe.

- *Timelessness.* As TS Eliot said, 'all time is eternally present.' The mystical experience feels as if it is outside time, and all change is seen as illusory.
- A spiritual sense of *self,* utterly different from the ordinary self with its consciousness, personality and will.

In addition to these I would also like to include:

- *Freedom.* We have seen with Krishnamurti that apart from free will and the burden of existential choice, there is also the carefree state of spiritual freedom. I believe this sense of release to be part of every mystical experience.
- *Joy.* Accompanying the sense of liberation during a mystical experience, there is normally a feeling of great joy at the union of the self (7) with the One (5), typically experienced as love.

Many writers on mysticism treat mystical experiences as rare episodes of 'religious experience' or epiphanies, often granting redemption or enlightenment in a sudden flash of understanding, after which one's life may be changed forever. Hence the emphasis on transiency – point (3) – by Happold. I have, however, endeavoured to introduce the mystical as part of everyday life, especially with regard to intuition, wherein the mystical can be functioning as an ongoing state of mind in the background of our consciousness. Moreover, if deep meditation qualifies as mystical experience then this would not be transient either. In these cases transiency would no longer be essential, or even typical.

Viewed thus, can we regard the physical activity practised by the Zen swordsman or Tolstoy's Levin as what we might call physical examples of mystical experience?

Let us consider point by point the items in Happold's list of characteristics.

Firstly, we have seen that Levin could not articulate his understanding, and that when the pupil tried to theorize about the skill of the Zen master he was always outmanoeuvred, thus this skill was (1) intrinsically *ineffable*. These contemplative physical activities also had (2) a *noetic* character since it is quite clear that the Zen master understood not only his own moves but those of the pupil, but not by means of any conceptual thoughts. Such a process in Levin was described by Tolstoy as being as if the scythe developed a consciousness of its own. *Transiency* (3) does not, however, seem to apply to such extended physical episodes, as was discussed above.

It was remarked that while the Zen master's actions are spiritually free (voluntary), they seem to be unwilled, because not orchestrated by conceptual thought. But if they are unwilled surely they are (4) *passive*, i.e. the swordsman is merely the instrument of master sword strokes that are, so to speak, executed through him. Likewise Levin was like a passive servant insofar as the scythe was 'mowing of itself, a body full of life and consciousness of its own.' Moreover, the Zen master does not consciously consider alternatives to his actions, for these would slow him down. Rather all the alternatives are united into an organic whole, and this guides his choices. Thus for him the swordplay is (5) an experience of *oneness*, uniting his own actions and the actions of his opponent.

When the Zen master plays his stroke, he has so much time that it feels (6) as if time is standing still, and that his stroke has a *timeless* inevitability. Like the eye of a storm, or 'the arbour where the rain beat', there is stillness and calm in the midst of frenetic activity.

Herrigel says technique only becomes master swordplay

when it becomes egoless and the pupil becomes detached 'not only from his opponent but from himself.' But still, *somebody* is selecting the sword stroke, and this somebody must be (7) his *higher self*, whether conceived as an entity or not. While the master's individual sword strokes are purposeless, and not specifically willed as the means to any end, they are still voluntary; they are spontaneous and (8) *freely* chosen, not by his will, but by his higher nature, whereas the pupil is in bondage to various thoughts and images. Finally, while no joy (9) is specifically mentioned in the Herrigel passage quoted, Tolstoy does record the moments when Levin's scythe mows of itself as: 'the most *blissful* moments.'

So it seems that something very far removed from silent meditation or religious epiphany can also provide a vehicle for mystical experience and that is: the dynamism of ritualized combat, and perhaps physical work generally. These seem to permit the operation of a bodily intelligence, different from the normal conceptual intelligence of the mind and its thoughts.

When we contrast these idyllic qualities of the mystical state with what Sartre would regard as the more realistic life choices defined by existentialism, the need for a rational justification of the mystical view becomes clear. For the reality of the human condition according to existentialism is the exact opposite of the characteristics itemized above. Instead of ineffability, the existentialist only permits herself options that are clearly conceivable in thought; she would regard any other kind of action as confused, and sadly deluded about any 'noetic' quality of insight. The 'authentic' agent is required to consciously take responsibility for every action: allowing herself to be the passive instrument of something unknown acting through her would also be regarded as self-delusion and not knowing her own mind. Far from life possessing a timeless unity, for her we are all trapped in the here and now in a meaningless succession of conflicts. Lastly, she sees her only existence in what she experiences consciously, where freedom not only fails to liberate but, on the contrary, is a form of bondage, experienced not as joy but as anguish.

How can we refute this position? We have seen with regard to creative manual skills how an alternative view is possible. But we shall find that a similarly rational account can also be provided for the abstract dilemmas of life, which may not necessarily exhibit any physical dexterity. For we shall see that the intelligent use of the mind can also employ a mystical element, independent of the use of the body. Indeed that normal cognition routinely employs such a mystical element. But if this is so, then we will of course need, as in the case of manual skills, an explanation of how and why it can be rational that by suspending thought one can nevertheless attain understanding. This surely is even more paradoxical in an environment purely of thought and reason than it is in the context of bodily movement. Furthermore, enlightenment would then be the realization of how the mystical is part of everyday life. In seeking the nature of enlightenment, therefore, our aim must be an overall rational understanding of the *nature* of the mystical in both the mental and the physical contexts. However, this must not be confused with the mystical understanding itself, any more than grasping the nature of enlightenment should be confused with enlightenment itself. For in each case, the former is definable logically, but the latter is not. Even if, for instance, spiritual freedom and spiritual identity are not definable logically, perhaps we shall nevertheless be able to define just *why* it is that they are not definable logically.

Chapter 3

The Self

Two kinds of comprehending

We continue our investigation of spiritual insight by now confining it to the purely mental sphere. Like Judaism, Christianity and Islam, Hinduism asserts the existence of a supreme being undetectable by the senses which, however, manifests itself not only in the physical world as *Brahman*, but also in the human mind as *Atman*:

> He who dwells in all beings but is separate from all beings, whom no being knows, whose body all beings are and who controls all beings from within – he the Self, is the Inner Ruler, the immortal.

This is from the Upanishads, the holy scriptures of ancient India, dating from 800 to 400 BC. Another Sanskrit text, the Kena Upanishad affirms that this being also regulates the human mind:

> At whose behest does the mind think? Who bids the body live? Who makes the tongue speak? Who is that effulgent Being that directs the eye to form and colour and the ear to sound? The Self is ear of the ear, mind of the mind, speech of speech... That which cannot be expressed in words but by which the tongue speaks – know that to be Brahman. Brahman is not the being who is worshipped by men. That which is not comprehended by the mind but by which the mind comprehends – know that to be Brahman. Brahman is not the being worshipped by men.

So, for Hinduism the Supreme Being is also the spiritual identity – or soul – of man and appears responsible for his cognitive functioning. But is this just a primitive prescientific causal theory of cognition, or a different kind of explanation altogether, a valid attempt at a non-causal explanation? Since Brahman is not an entity within the causal sequence, it cannot be the former. Whatever the case, we may at least feel that the above extract is logically consistent. However, the more we look at the text, the more we see this may not be so and that really Kena poses something of a logical riddle. For let us ask ourselves, by what means is this text itself meant to be understood? Clearly, the author believes he is telling us something important which we are being required to understand. But how are we meant to understand it?

Let us suppose we must understand Kena by means of our mind – for what other faculty is at our disposal? If this is the case, then it appears the author requires us to use our mind to understand sentences such as: *That which is not comprehended by the mind but by which the mind comprehends – know that to be Brahman.* In other words, we would be required to comprehend with our mind 'that which is not comprehended by the mind'. This is very puzzling, as it would require us to do the impossible, to mentally comprehend what cannot be comprehended. It would in fact be a self-contradictory requirement, and yet we are led to just such a contradiction if we assume that Kena is to be understood with our mind.

But, surely nothing can be literally explained, or understood, by means of a contradiction. To give meaning to the above text therefore, and avoid the contradiction, our only alternative would seem to be that Kena was intended to be understood *by a faculty other than the mind*. Now, since in the text that by which words are understood (including the words of Kena) is said to be the Self, perhaps the Self is intended to be just such an alternative faculty or mode of understanding. The text therefore appears to be hinting that the Self is a mode of understanding: a mode more basic or elemental than the conscious mind, which regulates all the cognitive functions which the mind performs. But what kind of understanding could this possibly be?

Endeavouring with Kena to interpret this cognitive role of the Self, let us firstly describe what is comprehended by the mind itself as *thoughts* (or perceptions). It then appears that the Self is intended to be what makes thoughts possible, without itself consisting of any thoughts. Now, Ludwig Wittgenstein, in his early work on logic, wrote about the limits of thought and referred to contradictory sentences as unthinkable. In like manner, perhaps we should say of the above text from Kena that, when interpreted by the mind, it is attempting to think the unthinkable, to say the unsayable. Wittgenstein proposed some merit in doing this, so as to identify the exact limits of thought:

> ... in order to be able to set a limit to thought, we should have to find both sides of the limit thinkable (i.e. we should have to be able to think what cannot be thought). It will therefore only be in language that the limit can be set and what lies on the other side of the limit will be nonsense.
>
> Ludwig Wittgenstein, *Tractatus Logico-Philosophicus*, Author's preface

But, as a matter of fact, Wittgenstein hinted that nonsense could sometimes be understood: by grasping in a different way what may nevertheless be 'shown' by an illogical sentence (such as those of Kena), even if nothing is actually 'said' by it. Perhaps a meaning similar to what Wittgenstein had in mind is being 'shown' by the text of Kena. For surely, despite the apparent contradiction, maybe we can't help feeling that we do understand Kena, which the author somehow manages to convey to us by other means, perhaps by some form of intuition which, so to speak, slips under our guard. It cannot of course be any thought 'said' or expressed by the text itself, since no thought is ever expressed by a contradiction.

Perhaps Kena was not, as we had assumed, attempting to

express a thought, and perhaps therefore was not trying to avoid a contradiction. Could it be that contradiction was its very purpose, and that in some sense its aim was for us to understand the contradiction itself? It may be, as Wittgenstein wrote, that what is beyond the limit of thought (e.g. contradictions) may, in some cases, convey understanding of a kind other than thought: and such a sentence may *show* this meaning, instead of *saying* it. This remains a conception quite alien to most other Western authors, as we shall see. For example Kena goes on to declare: *He only knows Brahman who knows him as beyond knowledge.* To Western thought this a straight contradiction: Brahman is being said to be both known and unknown. However, perhaps it may not be viewed as 'nonsense' if knowledge is being understood here in two different ways: on the one hand as conceptual thought, and on the other as something other than thought, but nevertheless a definite and useful experience (such as knowing a person). Then Kena might be construed as saying that Brahman is known only in this new sense, and not by conceptual thought in the mind.

Returning now to our original question: how were we intended to comprehend the more formidable sentence: *That which is not comprehended by the mind but by which the mind comprehends – know that to be Brahman.* My answer will only fully be given later, but it does seem clear that the question can only be answered by proposing some faculty of understanding other than thought. This is because we have already seen that attempting to comprehend this sentence by means of thoughts in the mind leads only to a contradiction. If the intention of Kena was indeed to convey, in this way, an understanding beyond the limits of language and thought, it nevertheless seems that Kena was concerned to speak literally and not say poetically in the manner of Lao Tzu and TS Eliot (Chapter 2). Rather, the author presents his thoughts as a prose narrative and seems intent on informing us of something important. And so, when the author says that Brahman cannot be comprehended by the mind, it appears he means this literally and not just symbolically. It is as if the very contradiction itself is the intended meaning, where perhaps this meaning is 'shown' by the contradiction, but not said by it.

But in that case, by what other mode of understanding may Kena possibly be understood? A fruitful alternative line of inquiry may be to ask what may have inspired the author of Kena to speak as he did, for one thing the author may have been alluding to is the experience of understanding obtained in deep meditation. In certain kinds of meditation, one of the most important aims is to rid the mind of all thoughts and perceptions. It follows that any form of insight or 'comprehending' one does attain in this state would certainly not consist of thoughts: in this case we might justifiably say such comprehending would not be by means of the 'mind', understood as a reasoning intellect. The use here of 'comprehending' would need to be justified rationally by its practical help in living. And maybe what Kena is attempting to do is to somehow provide thoughts about what can only properly be understood without thought during meditation, in order to imperfectly communicate some of the insights of private meditation verbally.

The result seems to be, however, that every such attempt to express these insights publicly in words inevitably requires us to flout the very laws of thought and reason that enable communication at all since, as we find in Kena, they result in contradictions. Perhaps indeed, this basic incompatibility was the original impetus to dispel all thoughts and images during meditation in the first place, viz: that the aim was, from the start, to understand in a manner contrary to the nature of thought. But if so, then the author of Kena should not have referred to Brahman as a being, for if Brahman is a being then it can be understood as such by the mind, we can have thoughts about that being; it is thinkable. And yet of course, we are told that Brahman cannot be comprehended by the mind, hence we cannot have thoughts about it. So if we want to avoid contradiction we must not refer to Brahman as a being. We shall now see how Buddhism, by contrast, retains the same aim of expressing some of the insight of meditation verbally, but avoids contradiction by referring only to the state of mind of the meditator, and not by referring this state to any independent being such as Brahman.

According to legend, the Buddha was born a wealthy prince, Siddhartha, in northern India, around 500 BC. He was moved to compassion for the suffering of humanity, and as a result, left his life of privilege for that of a wandering seeker after truth. Sitting one day under a Bodhi tree, he had an experience which has become celebrated as his Enlightenment. Part of the Buddha's insight, communicated subsequently, was that Brahman or Atman need not be an independent being encountered by the meditator, but that awareness of Brahman might just describe the meditator's own heightened state of consciousness. In other words, referring again to Kena, 'that by which the mind comprehends' need not be a being, but is rather a mode of understanding of which we become aware in enlightenment, and which makes perception and thought possible. This eliminates the particular contradiction of a *being* producing all possible understanding and perception, by means of which, however, that being could not itself be understood. For in Buddhism, there is just a higher state of consciousness (Enlightenment) grasping not only itself but also the operation of all lower states of consciousness (such as thought, perception). There is then, of course, no longer any contradiction in saying that thought or perception are unable to comprehend enlightenment, for that is a requirement of its very nature. Nevertheless, in consequence of this nature, it remains the case that any attempt to express enlightenment in words will, as with Brahman, break the laws of logic and language.

Buddhism employs spiritual practices such as meditation to induce enlightenment, and later, in China and Japan, Zen

Buddhism required contemplation of riddles or mystical koans (such as 'the sound of one hand clapping') to actively discourage rational analysis. But, more constructively, DT Suzuki cites a Zen master Tai-hui who used a bamboo stick for the following koan, saying, 'If you call this a stick, you affirm; if you call it not a stick, you negate. Beyond affirmation and negation what would you call it?' At another time Tai-hui said, 'The truth is not to be mastered by mere seeing, hearing, and thinking. If it is, it is no more than seeing, hearing and thinking; it is not at all seeking after the truth itself.'

Despite this, it remains our task to relate the use of such logical terms as 'truth', 'understanding', 'affirmation', 'negation' to the context of enlightenment. For we wish to specify exactly how what is experienced in meditation (or in reading enigmatic texts) is indeed a form of practical understanding, and not just a serene or mysterious state of mind. We saw how in martial arts and other physical activities the mystical could be construed as real understanding, because it conferred success in that activity in ways which thought and calculation were unable to do. We shall be asking similar cognitive questions of spirituality, in the sphere purely of abstract judgement, also.

The Buddha considered that he had provided a Middle Way between asserting the existence of a self (eternalism) and denying the existence of a self (nihilism), namely *understanding* of oneself, or self-awareness. This particular basic insight by the Buddha was that being self-aware need not mean there has to exist a being, the self, of which I must be aware. In other words, he transformed the meaning of the question. Perhaps some such Middle Way also provides the key to answering Tai-hui's generalized logical riddle, above. With respect to our own investigation of self-awareness, it is again not important to our account whether or not there exists a being, the soul. This is because we are interested only in the psychological reality of our spiritual identity and the part it plays in life. For it is possible to believe in a soul and yet not be self-aware, and certainly the possession or otherwise of such a belief by a person is of no relevance or interest for our investigation. Equally, a Buddhist may not believe in a soul, but be highly self-aware, and this would be very relevant to our inquiry.

Christian mystics

In the West, medieval Christian contemplatives have raised similar questions about our understanding of union with God. To signify its ambivalent nature, they have referred to it in such terms as the desert, the cloud of unknowing, or the divine darkness. These metaphors certainly seem to conflict with the Eastern metaphor of enlightenment. However, it seems they were used primarily to distinguish the obscurity of the earthly experience from its dazzling counterpart, experienced only in heaven. Furthermore, these terms are used, not to signify obscurity alone, but also to signify successful avoidance of the perceived misleading nature of clear thought. For the anonymous author of *The Cloud of Unknowing* wrote:

> ... but of God Himself no man can think. And therefore, I would leave all that thing that I can think, and choose to love that thing that I cannot think. For why; He may be well loved, but not thought. By love may He be gotten and holden; but by thought never.

The implication seems to be not that there is no clarity concerning the author's desired mental state, indeed his experience is very clear, but that the clarity is not one of thought.

St Teresa of Avila, the sixteenth century abbess of a Spanish Carmelite monastery, wrote extensively, and with great exactitude, on the nature of contemplative prayer. In particular, she considered the question of whether or not divine union might be said to constitute a form of understanding:

Thus does God, when he raises a soul to union with himself, suspend the natural action of all her faculties. She neither sees, hears nor understands, so long as she is united with God... If you, nevertheless, ask how it is possible that the soul can see and understand that she has been in God, since during the union she has neither sight nor understanding, I reply that she does not see it then, but that she sees it clearly later, after she has returned to herself, not by any vision, but by a certitude which abides with her and which God alone can give her.

St Teresa of Avila, *The Interior Castle, Fifth Abode*

Teresa's explanation resembles my hypothesis about Kena being a recollection of Hindu meditation, and even of TS Eliot's memory of the timeless moment viz: they require processes of thought or time respectively, in order to be expressed or experienced. Therefore, despite such distracting words as 'unknowing' and 'divine darkness', it is likely that, being mystical experiences, these all do contain a noetic element of some kind. But according to Teresa, if divine union provides a form of understanding, it seems to be the partial understanding now that we were previously united to something we did not then understand. Thus there is an element both of understanding and of not understanding; it is this that can trip us into self-contradiction when we attempt to describe it. In the divine darkness therefore it seems to be the current understanding that describes it as divine, while the earlier non-understanding provides the necessary darkness.

But perhaps we understood God, not by the ordinary mind, but by a special contemplative 'comprehending'. Teresa also attempted to answer directly the question as to what, if anything, it is that is comprehended during union with God. In the following text cited by William James, it is important to distinguish her employment of 'understands' which is used to describe the ordinary mind, and 'comprehends' which is used specifically to describe that understanding, if any, attendant upon divine union.

> If our understanding comprehends, it is in a mode which remains unknown to it, and it can understand nothing of what it comprehends. For my own part, I do not believe that it does comprehend, because, as I said, it does not understand itself to do so. I confess it is all a mystery in which I am lost.

If one bears this distinction in mind, the clouds of confusion should disperse, revealing a carefully constructed thought. Teresa is saying that the mind does not have any conception of a mode of comprehending our union with God. If there is such a mode, she is saying it must be one that is unknown to the ordinary thinking mind (*it can understand nothing of what it comprehends*). For this reason she does not really believe there is any such mode of mentally comprehending our contemplative union with God. Nevertheless, one can't help feeling that she wishes she could comprehend the divine union, that she feels there is something there to be comprehended, if only because it affects her life subsequently, and she confesses herself lost in its mystery.

This is not inconsistent with the earlier passage, in which she remarked that the soul can in the present understand that she was previously united with God, for this said nothing about any special 'comprehending' during the contemplative union itself, but only denied any understanding of it by the ordinary mind at that time.

Modern doubts

But surely a similar question arises for all of us: what is that special kind of inward understanding or comprehending of ourself that cannot be expressed in thought, but has been so widely debated, both East and West? Most of us lack the certitude expressed by Teresa, and one can perhaps sympathize at this point with the frustration expressed by a modern spiritual seeker:

> Spiritual life is as natural as breathing. All you have to do is still the mind, open your heart and step into the flow of universal love. It's very near, nearer than your own heartbeat. Freedom is in the present moment, here and now; nothing could be simpler. Just listen to the still, small voice in the centre of your being, and all your problems will vanish like the dew in the morning.
>
> That's the punchline.
>
> So simple, and yet so very elusive! Some of us find ourselves in a very unhappy predicament. We know the punchline, and we believe it's true, but all our efforts to step on the Path meet with dismal failure; concentrating on the here and now is far from blissful, so obviously we're not doing it properly. There's a block to the 'higher Self' we hear and read so much about, and to add to the bafflement and frustration we are told, gently and patiently, that we put the block there ourselves. There's a strong hint, again in the nicest possible way, that the block has to do with thinking too much.
>
> Viv Mitchell, *A Spiritual Predicament* (*unpublished*)

It is plain that the obscurity of spiritual classics such as the Upanishads or the Christian mystics which we have been discussing renders their explanations inadequate for many sceptical modern minds. But there is more to it than that: the problem is, as Mitchell says, an elusive one, for it rests upon the whole way we approach such questions, the nature of the intellectual resources we bring to bear. Are we going to let a contradiction quash our understanding? Can we trust our intuition? That is the kind of question that has to be faced, and it is in that sense that we 'put the block there ourselves', not letting ourself 'step on the Path'. For example, the present moment only becomes blissful if it is *viewed* timelessly (q.v. TS Eliot, Chapter 2) for bliss is clearly not intrinsic to the moment itself. But if we can't help viewing it as 'involved with past and future', then of course the present moment becomes humdrum and may be 'far from blissful'. Mitchell is not a sceptic; rather hers is a heartfelt plea to be provided with thoughts about how to comprehend in the manner of St Teresa or the Kena Upanishad. But we have seen from our examination of these texts and from Buddhism that this is precisely what cannot be done, since it is the impossibility of rendering them in thought that makes them so special and sanctifies their subject matter. Similarly, there can be no mere thoughts telling us how to experience the present moment as timeless. 'Thinking too much' is therefore indeed the problem.

Nevertheless, it is the declared aim of this book to clarify this obscurity by explaining, in a form resistant to modern criticism, how it might be possible to 'comprehend' other than by under-standing, i.e. to comprehend in a manner other than thought. We shall, in other words, justify in thought exactly how *there can be* a kind of comprehending different from thought, without actually defining it in thought. For if we could do the latter, then such comprehending would just amount to another kind of thought.

Meister Eckhart

We have seen how Hinduism and Buddhism both say there is a mystical element at the heart of human cognition. This is a statement about human experience, namely that perception or the acquisition of knowledge cannot be adequately understood by thought and reason alone, but only by means of another faculty of understanding. This faculty cannot be put into words or conceived in thought for the very reason that it is the basis by which words and thoughts are themselves understood. In concert with Kena therefore, I am suggesting that the nature of intelli-gence cannot be grasped only by means of the products of intel-ligence, but that something more is needed. The name given to this additional mystical element was the Self or Enlightenment which, being the basis of the rational mind, can now also be seen as the origin of human intelligence. We shall later clarify this claim, demonstrating how this origin of intelligence can be both mystical, and therefore inexplicable, and at the same time intelligible.

The fourteenth century German Christian contemplative, Meister Eckhart, shared a mystical view of the self that was similar in many ways to Eastern views. However, he crystallized this more by providing an exact reason why the self or soul cannot be comprehended by ideas in the mind, namely that all such ideas must be produced by the soul from sense perceptions:

> But an idea, so received, necessarily comes in from outside, through the senses. Thus the soul knows about everything but itself. There is an authority who says that the soul can neither conceive nor admit any idea of itself. Thus it knows about everything else but has no self-knowledge, for ideas always enter through the senses and therefore the soul cannot get an idea of itself. Of nothing does the soul know so little as it knows of itself, for lack of means.
> Meister Eckhart, *The Sermons*

But the strange thing is that Eckhart seems quite unconcerned about the soul's ignorance about itself. Clearly he believes the soul *really* does know about itself – just not by means of ideas. Why is Eckhart so confident that he does indeed have a soul? As with the Hindu thinkers, he must believe he has a means of knowing his soul (or his soul has a means of knowing itself), other than by ideas or thoughts. Notice here though that unlike our discussion of Kena, Eckhart's rejection of the idea of a soul is not due to any inconsistency in the idea itself, but is due rather to the 'lack of means' whereby such an idea could be produced.

However, a question for us now has to be: given the lack of any idea of the self, how would Eckhart explain to a modern doubter like Mitchell (with her 'block to the higher Self') the basis for his certainty? Indeed Eckhart even goes on to make a virtue of the soul's ignorance of itself for he immediately adds, 'And that indicates that within itself the soul is free, innocent of all instrumentalities and ideas, and that is why God can unite with it, he, too, being without idea or likeness.' In other words, it is the soul's complete inconceivability that makes it *free* (recall that this was what Krishnamurti had also been saying in Chapter 1), and the soul's ignorance, like the cloud of unknowing, is evidently viewed, perversely, as a source of knowledge about itself, and about God.

As with Eastern meditation, it seems that for Eckhart it is the act of contemplation itself that put him, he believed, in contact with his soul. But if the soul is an entity or 'being' then its characteristics (such as immortality) surely constitute states of affairs; how then can a state of affairs be represented or expressed other than by means of a thought or idea? In other words, we are entitled to ask why Eckhart's proposed soul is not simply an illusion; why does he believe that contemplation is a route to knowledge? If there is any knowledge of states of affairs, apart from ideas, this will surely need to be demonstrated and justified.

Descartes

In 17ᵗʰ century France, a secular philosopher, Rene Descartes, who was influenced by the new methods of the Renaissance, pioneered a revolution in Western philosophy. Where Eckhart and other medieval church scholastics had assumed the possibility of contemplatively knowing the soul independently of thought and ideas, Descartes questioned this, and effectively exposed the weakness of such assumptions. Impressed by the emerging science of Galileo and other Renaissance experimenters, Descartes sought to employ the new methods of acquiring knowledge to the human mind itself. By applying a method of systematic doubt to everything he thought he knew, he aimed to discover whether there was anything which was immune from doubt, and so could be said to be known with absolute certainty.

As the first rule of his method of doubt he vowed 'to accept as true nothing that I did not know to be evidently so... and to apply my judgements to nothing but that which showed itself so clearly and distinctly to my mind that I should never have occasion to doubt it.' We can see that this immediately eliminates Eckhart's knowledge of the soul, since only ideas are clear and distinct, and for Eckhart knowledge of the soul was 'dark' and independent from ideas. With this epistemological method Descartes engineered a sharp break with all previous Western philosophy which, up to then, had mainly been about what exists rather than about our knowledge of what exists. As such, Descartes is widely regarded as the founder of modern philosophy, and his legacy is responsible for the existence and methods of all the modern human and social sciences such as psychology, sociolinguistics, anthropology, in which man is known only via ideas and concepts which define him.

But while the method of Descartes dispensed with the contemplative medieval soul, in favour of ideas that were clear and distinct, he found that there was instead a different concept of the self, of whose existence he could be absolutely certain. By systematically doubting whether he were dreaming or awake, whether he was made of flesh and blood and so forth, he arrived at one belief it was impossible for him to doubt, namely the fact that he existed. He expressed this as a famous inference: *I think therefore I exist*, Cogito ergo sum. For the moment he began to doubt if he existed, the very process of doubting would itself bring him into existence. It is clear that for Descartes the self is now synonymous with the thinker or, more generally, with the subject of conscious experiences, for from all of these experiences, thought Descartes, his existence could equally be inferred. We have been all along calling this the lower self, and it is our concern now to establish whether any higher spiritual identity may also be said to survive the Cartesian process of systematic doubt.

It is often not emphasized that Descartes also interpreted the Cogito to mean its converse, for he also said, 'I see very clearly and distinctly that in order to exist, one must think'; in other words, if I exist, then I think, or in his own words:

> I am, I exist: that is certain. But for how long? For as long as I think. If I ceased to think, I might very well cease to be, or to exist, at that moment.

The reason Descartes believes this would seem to be his belief that all knowledge comprises clear and distinct ideas, i.e. thoughts. Therefore, my only way of knowing anything is by thinking. But if all knowledge comprises thoughts, then when I am not thinking I have *no way of knowing* whether or not I exist. But why should this mean that I actually do not exist? Descartes was here drawing a metaphysical conclusion, a conclusion about what can exist, from an epistemic premise, a premise about what can be known. Descartes' faith in his method appears to be such that, if it is impossible for an object to be detected by his method, then that object cannot exist. This seems to anticipate principles introduced only later by empiricism, in which existence and truth are directly linked to the possibility of knowledge. It is for this reason that Descartes is viewed as the father of modern philosophy: by shifting the priority from the nature of what is real, to the grounds for knowing it, he replaced metaphysics by epistemology as the cornerstone of Western philosophy.

Thus, from the impossibility of knowing whether he exists when he is not thinking, Descartes infers that he actually does not exist when he is not thinking. He then slips imperceptibly into describing himself as 'a substance whose whole essence or nature consists in thinking'; he was *ens cogitans,* a thinking thing and nothing else. Thus, from the mere fact that he exists he inferred something about his nature, from his existence he inferred his essence; in other words, from epistemology he was drawing a metaphysical conclusion. Now was this conclusion warranted? Plainly, to neither Eckhart nor St Teresa was thinking believed to be necessary in order for the soul to exist, since they could contemplatively experience their soul in the absence of thought. Indeed, Teresa attested that any such comprehending suspended the natural action of all her faculties (including thought), and Eckhart admitted his knowledge of the soul did not employ any ideas, i.e. thoughts. So either this experience of self by Teresa and Eckhart was illusory since the only knowledge is thought, or the metaphysical inference by Descartes, that his essence amounted purely to thought, was not justified, since there are other ways of knowing the self. What Descartes seems certainly to have been asserting, in contrast with medieval scholastics, was that anything that cannot be conceived in thought cannot possibly exist, because it cannot possibly be known. Consequently, he was denying, in effect, that we can have any higher nature or essence that is independent of our thoughts and perceptions. Our existence is defined wholly by our thoughts, and any other identity or essence we give ourself must be based upon this. The moral and personal implications of this view by later Cartesians that 'existence precedes essence' were to be explored in our own day by Sartre (Chapter 1), Beckett and others as existentialism.

However, was Descartes right about the *cogito?* Even in the widest sense of 'think' embracing perceptions and emotions, it may not be true that 'in order to exist, one must think'. For, without necessarily contemplating the divine, we can instead consult a faculty even more basic than thinking, namely consciousness. The first thing to notice about this faculty is that to be conscious, it is not necessary to think; for example if, when meditating, one succeeds in eliminating all thoughts and images from the mind then by definition one is not thinking. And yet one remains fully conscious, perhaps on a higher plane of consciousness, but that doesn't matter at this stage; all that matters is the fact that we can be fully conscious while not thinking or experiencing anything. But it is not true to say, while in this state, that we do not *know* or understand anything; indeed the whole purpose of meditation is to increase our understanding and to become self-aware, *including awareness of our own existence*. The same applies to any mystical experience manifesting any or all of the characteristics: passivity, oneness, freedom, timelessness etc. mentioned in Chapter 2; in any such mystical experience we are not thinking, but we are profoundly aware of existing. None of these characteristics of mystical experience constitute thoughts or feelings, however, in the ordinary sense intended by Descartes.

But disregarding mystical experience or meditation, it suffices to point out that consciousness is *logically prior* to thought, by which we mean simply that one can be conscious without thinking, but one cannot think without being conscious. And it seems, contrary to Descartes, that one of the things we can know by pure consciousness alone, without the intervention of any thought, is that we exist. The point was well put by an unknown medieval contemplative, describing those who fail to grasp this:

Because they are blind they mistakenly call this simple teaching 'intellectual subtlety', whereas if only they were to look at it properly they would find it to be a straightforward, easy lesson for simple people. For the only man I can think of who would be too stupid or ignorant for this would be the man incapable of recognizing that he existed: ignorant *not* of what he is, so much as *that* he is. Clearly it is as natural for the most ignorant cow or unintelligent animal (can we or can we not say that one creature is more stupid and unintelligent than another?) to be aware of its own existence. Then it is much more likely that man, who alone of the animal kingdom has been endowed with reason, should recognize his own existence!
Anonymous, *The Epistle of Privy Council*

Since Cartesians only accept clear and distinct ideas as the mark of knowledge, it seems that whatever is known by pure consciousness (or the 'cloud of unknowing') would have to be dismissed by them as ideas that are obscure or confused, and hence not really knowledge at all, or else ideas of great 'intellectual subtlety'. Ironically, this includes some of the most obvious facts, such as the fact of one's own existence. However, the latter does seem to entail that recognition of such a fact is not a thought, since while animals both know they exist and may also sometimes think, they nevertheless do not think about such abstractions as their own existence. Animals may well know they exist but, unlike Descartes, this never consists in them thinking that they exist.

David Hume

Before attempting to resolve this dilemma, we first consider one further development of the philosophy of Descartes, namely empiricism. The empiricists believed that all ideas were obtained only by means of sense-impressions, and about 100 years after Descartes a Scottish empiricist philosopher, David Hume, argued that we can have no idea of a self, and therefore no knowledge of it. Accepting the Cartesian premise that all knowledge comprises ideas or thoughts, he famously went on to deny that these thoughts required a thinker; there is no self at all, merely the occurrences of the ideas themselves. For, he said:

> For my part, when I enter most intimately into what I call *myself*, I always stumble on some particular perception or other, of heat or cold, light or shade, pain or pleasure. I never catch *myself* at any time without a perception, and never can observe anything but the perception. When my perceptions are removed for any time, as by sound sleep, so long am I insensible of *myself*, and may truly be said not to exist.
>
> David Hume, *A Treatise of Human Nature*

But this again neglects the experience of pure consciousness provided either by meditation, or by contemplative prayer (recall that Eckhart had agreed 400 years earlier that all ideas come via the senses, but had not denied the existence of the soul). Let us therefore in the light of these considerations attend carefully to what Hume said.

Firstly, it is clear that *entering intimately into myself* does not include the practice of meditation, for if it did then I would not continually 'stumble on some particular perception or other', since meditation is the elimination of perceptions. And yet, prima facie, the very purpose of meditation is in order to enter most intimately into what I call *myself*. Clearly it can only do this if the resulting self-awareness does not consist of ideas, in other words, provided that self-knowledge need not always consist in thinking.

Similarly with *I never can catch myself at any time without a perception*. If by 'catching' Hume meant perceiving, then his statement was tautologously true, since the 'catching' would itself bring the perception into existence. But if he simply meant being aware of oneself, then it is false since we can be aware of ourself without a perception, namely during meditation. However, like Descartes, Hume implies that self-awareness is, in any case, only *possible* via ideas, for he says that 'in sound sleep' he may 'truly be said not to exist'. It seems he believed that to be awake is to be thinking or perceiving. But whereas Descartes allowed for the same self to come in and out of existence as thoughts and perceptions came and went, Hume dispensed with this, saying we are simply the thoughts and perceptions themselves. He declared that no continuing self exists and that we are nothing but 'a bundle or collection of different perceptions'. However, it is plain that during meditation 'perceptions are removed' for a time, and yet in this case I am not 'insensible of myself', and may well know myself to exist, quite apart from these perceptions.

Finally, since Hume viewed his introspections as constituting an empirical inquiry, it seems we may object even on his own terms that he did not avail himself of sufficient 'empirical' data for this purpose viz: the data concerning meditation, data which demonstrate that we can indeed be aware of ourself other than by thoughts and perceptions.

Kena, by contrast, seemed to say we possess a self, Brahman, other than the mind, that enables us to understand the mind by other means. Thus, like Eckhart's soul, this self was not itself built from mental contents such as sights and sounds (Hume's perceptions), but had the power to enable sounds to be heard ('ear of the ear') and sights to be seen ('eye of the eye'). For Hume of course there was nothing else that enabled sense-impressions to be experienced, for these sense-impressions themselves were taken as primitive and irreducible. Eckhart had also said that the soul, which was not an idea from the senses, nevertheless *enabled the senses to operate* so as to create ideas. In other words for Eckhart, the soul, which cannot itself be known by ideas but was known only contemplatively, nevertheless enabled the senses to construct ideas.

Of course, according to Descartes and Hume, no such contemplative faculty or entity can be known, since only ideas themselves can be known, not any posited indefinable entities or powers to create such ideas. Such entities and powers, because they are not conceived by ideas, must therefore be regarded as meaningless notions. However, it will be argued later that there is a way of understanding ourself other than by ideas, and so the paradox that we cannot understand the very mental processes responsible for creating our own ideas will be removed. This indeed is the position adopted by Buddhism, for in Buddhism the fact of self-awareness when perceiving, say a flower, is not taken to require the idea of a self, but rather becoming aware of the flower in a different kind of way. This enhanced sense of self during perception is regarded as one of the characteristics of enlightenment.

Chapter 4

Loss of Self

We have been examining some of the theoretical differences between Eastern and Western accounts of the self. We now consider the far-reaching consequences of these theoretical differences for our practical experience of life. In Buddhism, for instance, we find an analysis of personal and perceptual experience, just as deep and just as wide-ranging and analytical as Western phenomenology, that was so meaningful that it had actually become a way of life for millions of people, unbeknownst to Hume and Descartes, for over a thousand years. It is informative to consider how this practical Buddhist analysis of experience differs, therefore, from the practical impact of the Western philosophical tradition.

The human mind is the same all over the world and we might expect the products of careful introspection to have been the same in Asia as they were in Europe. However, interestingly, this was not the case because Buddhists on the whole managed to avoid the nihilistic/negative consequences of failing to find the self, which befell the West. Instead, this very vacancy itself led them in the opposite direction, towards a new kind of personal rediscovery. But this discovery did not consist in finding something, a self, accompanying all our perceptions, as the Kena Upanishad had affirmed. Although we have been speaking all along of self-expression and how to comprehend the self, Buddhism talks not of this, but instead emphasizes a meaningful sidelining of the self. Consider the words of a modern Buddhist:

> So I, this strong, self-conscious feeling of I, is the cause of suffering and needs to be brought to an end, No-I, to restore the balance and

alleviate suffering.

The Venerable Myokyo-ni, *Introducing Buddhism*

What is this 'strong self-conscious feeling of I'? It is how I appear to myself. People often call this the ego but an ego is really a dominant self-image, and that is something more extreme than what we are considering here. An ego is due to what Sartre called 'bad faith' (Chapter 1), but not everybody is an egotist, not everybody manifests bad faith, but we all have the 'strong self-conscious feeling of I' even, or especially, Sartre's authentic individual. It is to do with my consciousness of my purposes, thoughts, intentions, emotions, roles, sympathies, personality, desires. This is what is meant by my experiences, and me as a subject of possible experience. It means all my mental content, including myself as the owner of this content, as defined for example by the Cartesian thinker (or by the apperceptive unity of Immanuel Kant). Well, David Hume said there is no such owner of all this content. But if there is no such owner, how come I think that there is, namely *me*? By this we mean that there is still a need to define how our very real sense of self originates. Recall that the method used by Descartes – 'I think therefore I am' – had the drawback that were I to stop thinking (or feeling) then I would cease to exist. Yet this fails to agree with our ongoing sense of self, which does not go out of existence, but seems to persist as long as we remain conscious, whether thinking or not.

Rather than a sense of ego, it is the Cartesian thinker that seems to correspond to the 'strong self-conscious feeling of I' rejected by Buddhism. In apparent agreement with Hume, they are denying that the Cartesian-I really exists. However, they are really affirming a higher sense of self which, since it is not given by self-conscious thought, is now referred to as No-I. So we can clarify by saying that one of the many things Buddhists mean by 'I' is Cartesian (or Kantian) self-consciousness, myself only as author of my thoughts and subject of my perceptions.

Nevertheless, I have implied that what they mean by No-I is not something as negative as the Humean lack of self, and indeed may be the opposite of it.

Recalling now the philosophy of Jean-Paul Sartre: like Descartes, Sartre accepted his existence as a given, and defined his essence from it ('existence precedes essence'). This view is very different from Buddhism since Sartre regards the existence of 'I' not as an illusion, but as the unpalatable truth. However, there seem to be some similarities, for Sartre appears to confirm the suffering identified by Myokyo-ni. This is because, for existentialists, not only the exponents of bad faith suffer, but even the most authentic individuals suffer anguish at their *freedom* in attempting to acknowledge all the options that really exist for them.

But what is the suffering referred to by Myokyo-ni? Classically, Buddhism refers to 'grasping' or 'attachments' as the source of all suffering (second Noble Truth of Buddhism). But I believe here a case can also be made for identifying it with existential angst, just as in Judaism (Chapter 1) we identified this angst with the symbolic wandering of the Israelites lost in the Sinai Desert, as well as with their bondage in Egypt. We may perhaps justify such an identification in the current context, by noting that both Myokyo-ni and Sartre are attributing the suffering partly to the self-conscious burden of choices. But while they may be agreed on the problem, they are by no means agreed on the solution. We have seen that for Sartre there is no solution: it is simply the human condition. But for Myokyo-ni the solution resides in No-I.

Now, what does Myokyo-ni say about No-I? She says in the same text that it is 'inconceivable to I'. This seems logical because since it is not self-consciousness then it is not defined by the process of thinking, nor by any of the thoughts thought by I, and so not by any of the concepts conceived by I. So it must be inconceivable. Where Hume empirically searched experience and failed to find the self, in the Buddhist scriptures, the *Abhidharma* (commentaries on the original sutras of the Buddha), Buddhism endeavours to deduce the *impossibility* of a thinkable self. Sartre demonstrated the same thing, for if existence precedes essence then no human essence or real self can be *conceivable*. This is because if every human action had to conform to this essence, we would never be able to conceive or imagine acting to the contrary. But we always can, and to pretend otherwise is bad faith. It is this, says Sartre, that is the anguish of human freedom.

But if an understanding of the sense of self given by No-I cannot result from any thoughts or concepts we have about ourself, then it must come from a different kind of understanding altogether: enlightenment. This is not an option available to existentialism or to Hume, since what cannot be conceived in thought cannot, following Descartes, be understood at all, and must be meaningless. Nevertheless, during meditation we can experience a sense of self when not perceiving at all, hence this self-awareness must be independent from any perceptions it may subsequently accompany.

According to Buddhism, true liberation, as opposed to Sartre's freedom, consists in shedding our confinement by thought, and accepting a sense of self independent of thought, imbued by Buddhist spiritual practice, namely by acknowledging the Four Noble Truths, and following the Noble Eightfold Path. Enigmatically, it is this very sense of self that Myokyo-ni calls No-I since, while the spiritual practice aims at self-awareness, it nevertheless shuns any concept of a self. Indeed, the attainment of self-awareness is described as nothing other than a state of understanding or enlightenment. The experience of No-I is therefore not only not an experience of self-consciousness, it is not an experience of any conceivable self whatsoever, but only an experience of understanding oneself. No-I is not therefore surreptitiously just another idea of self under the name 'No-I' instead of 'I', although it is admittedly an idea. Rather it is the idea of what it is to understand oneself without possessing an idea of oneself. Notice how this differs from Sartre's idea of the authentic individual, which really was just an alternative idea of oneself, since it was the idea of a person who thinks and acts in certain 'authentic' ways, rather than other ways. Recall (Chapter 1) that this meant acknowledging all the choices that really exist for one, instead of conveniently ignoring some of them. Sartre saw this as being existentially free; but is it *spiritual* freedom?

The East/West divide

No liberating notion akin to No-self prevailed in the West, only the concept of a soul, and this had become compromised by science. As a result, the Cartesian cogito, due to its apparently scientific basis, was subsequently to have a profound effect on man's conception of himself. The faith of medieval times in the soul came increasingly to be ignored or discredited, and the resulting self-doubt led to crises of confidence so that ultimately, for many people, life came gradually to lose much of the meaning it once had.

It is also largely as a result of Descartes that there is today a schism between Eastern and Western philosophy. The West now accepts as knowledge only what can be conceived in thought or perceived, while the East has long believed the deepest knowledge can be neither conceived in thought nor perceived by the senses, but can only be attained by the blankness of meditation. This amounts to a conflict concerning the very nature of what is meant by self-knowledge. On the one hand, meditators and contemplatives feel we grasp not only our existence, but a sense of our inmost essence, independently of all ideas or thoughts, even though many like Eckhart admitted they were unable to explain how this can be possible. On the other hand the modern sceptic can only understand ideas and perceptions, and cannot understand a mere blank. On the face of it this does not seem unreasonable; what could be more reasonable than to deny meaning to what is declared to be intrinsically inexpressible? This is particularly credible since describing the inexpressible always runs the risk of appearing to express it. Bertrand Russell wrote, concerning Wittgenstein's declarations about the inexpressible: 'What causes hesitation is the fact that, after all, Mr Wittgenstein manages to say a good deal about what cannot be said.' One reply might be that self-awareness has been declared inexpressible only in terms of conceptual thought ('ideas'), but perhaps self-expression is possible in other ways, and may be grasped by means of a different kind of mental functioning, such as intuition. Such a self would then be more than the mere 'thinking thing' of Descartes. Of course, the nature of intuition would then need to be clarified.

The Cartesian self is seemingly what is depicted by the tramp in the cartoon of Chapter 1. For the factual information at the desk is nothing but the expression of various thoughts, and a person who seeks his identity in these terms evidently sees himself, like Descartes, in terms of thoughts and nothing more. Surely, the humour of the cartoon derives from what Camus called the absurdity of seeing ourselves this way, in other words the absurdity of the Cartesian thesis. But perhaps it is, rather, the deadpan humour of the mirthless kind which Samuel Beckett made his speciality: mirthless because only the bare bones of an identity are being offered by the pedantic desk clerk inside each of us. Mirthless too, because of the seemingly inescapable logic of Descartes and Hume that, however absurd this view of man may seem, it is nevertheless the truth. Our spiritual identity has vanished, and instead at our very centre there is now just a Void.

Like the tramp, Tolstoy's Levin (Chapter 2) found thought and reason a very thin coat to wear against the chill winds of life, meaning perhaps that thought and reason preserve our existence, but leave us impoverished in joy or fulfilment, so that such a life is no longer worth living. Descartes lets us know that we exist, but not that we are *alive*. Our spiritual identity has become replaced by endless thoughts, as this is now our only way of understanding the world. As a result, mental life becomes reduced to a stream of consciousness and contains nothing more; an example might be the following from James Joyce:

> Where was the chap I saw in that picture somewhere? Ah, in the dead sea, floating on his back, reading a book with a parasol open. Couldn't sink if you tried: so thick with salt. Because the weight of the water, no, the weight of the body in the water is equal to the weight of the. Or is it the volume is equal of the weight? It's a law something like that.
> James Joyce, *Ulysses*, p. 73

If there is such a thing as intuition, it is not presented by these half-formed thoughts and random associations of an average human mind, with no requirement for it to be rational or its memories to be accurate. In particular, it is tacitly implied that there is no content of consciousness above or beyond the kind of thing that is written here. There is nothing to read between the lines; there is no higher sense of Self; although from the content and ordering of the thoughts and feelings we may perhaps be able to attribute character, personality or motives to the thinker. We also may gain the impression that the only point to such a life is the avoidance of boredom, by endlessly catching at new experiences. Descartes and Hume tell us there are only these concrete experiences, and when they stop, we cease to exist. For Descartes the self comes and goes with experiences and hence is fragmentary; for Hume the self does not exist at all. These beliefs create a very real fear of experience ceasing, for it is the fear of nonexistence. The fear of even momentary separation from thought was tellingly expressed by Beckett:

> I've looked everywhere, there must be someone, the voice must

belong to someone, I've no objection, what it wants I want, I am it,
I've said so, it says so, from time to time it says so, then it says not,
I've no objection, I want it to go silent, it wants to go silent, it can't,
it does for a second, then it starts again, that's not the real silence, it
says that's not the real silence, what can be said of the real silence, I
don't know, that I don't know what it is, that there is no such thing,
that perhaps there is such a thing, that perhaps there is somewhere,
I'll never know.
Samuel Beckett, *The Unnameable*

Here, the eponymous 'Unnameable' is perhaps the Soul in the
silence reported by Eckhart and St Teresa. The voice, by contrast,
is the Cartesian thinker with which, on the one hand, the
Unnameable initially fails to identify, and treats as someone else
('the voice must belong to someone'). On the other hand, he
grudgingly accepts that he always wants what it wants, so he
must be the same as the voice and admits 'I am it'. This amounts
to a reluctant acceptance of the Cartesian theory that we are
nothing more than the thinkers of our thoughts. At the same time
there are moments when he escapes from the accompanying
voice, and gets the idea that he can exist apart from the voice,
and these are the momentary silences or gaps between his
thoughts. However, what he really wants is to experience the real
(i.e. lasting) silence; but the voice by definition can't go silent for
any significant period.

In this endeavour, he surely resembles a man attempting to
meditate but failing repeatedly, because he keeps being interrupted by his own thoughts (the voice). The reason he keeps
interrupting himself is surely because he fears that during the
silence he may cease to exist, since he will have no way of
knowing he exists. But why does he believe this? It is because he
believes, with Descartes, that the only way of knowing he exists
is by thought, since thought is *the only way of knowing anything at
all*. The result is that when he momentarily stops thinking (the

voice goes silent 'for a second') it is only because he is in a state of readiness or preparedness for the next thought. Thus the gaps in his thoughts are not the real silence because they consist in *waiting* for thought, and this is really an attenuated form of thought; so this silence is a false one. Beckett is surely conveying what it feels like to be clinging to thought because one is afraid to genuinely stop thinking; he feels that his desire for silence conflicts with his need for existence. We may alternatively say that, as described in the Introduction, the Unnameable feels he is 'in conflict with life as a whole.' For the silence of his 'inmost being' appears to clash with the demands of existence – which requires only his thoughts and perceptions.

By contrast, here is Krishnamurti again describing the real silence that can be attained in successful meditation:

> Meditation is an intensification of the mind which is in the fullness of silence. The mind is not still like some tamed, frightened or disciplined animal; it is still as the waters are still many fathoms down. The stillness there is not like that on the surface when the winds die. This stillness has a life and a movement of its own, which is related to the outer flow of life, but is untouched by it.

Comparing this with the passage from Beckett, the surface of the water is like the interface between the mind and the world, and the waves produced by the wind are the direct effects of the world on the mind in the form of perceptions, feelings and thoughts; they react with alacrity or resistance to stimuli, like an animal being disciplined. The occasional surface stillness 'when the winds die' is like Beckett's momentary silences of the gaps between thoughts: they are intrinsically unstable and are only waiting for the next gust. For Beckett this is the entirety of conscious mental life: as insubstantial as wavelets being teased by the wind. But for Krishnamurti consciousness also has its own deep currents, which we can liken to intuitions, and which are not dependent upon sense-experiences on the surface.

The root problem for Beckett's Unnameable and for all of us would seem to be, therefore, to justify a mental state such as meditation in rational terms that the thinker can understand. This in turn means to formulate in conceptual thought a way of understanding or knowing *other than by conceptual thought*. For only by such a way of knowing can we, when not thinking, still know or understand ourself to continue to exist, and thus experience the real silence. And only by formulating this in thought can we, after experiencing this real silence rather than the false silence, then go on to describe the difference to the thinker. This of course would be to find a way of conceiving pure *consciousness* as itself a mode of understanding, since we are all, even without meditation, conscious of our existence prior to thought. The main function of meditation here is just to eliminate thought, so that we can then more easily recognize our own consciousness.

What is a thought?

In order to examine further what aspects of meditation can and cannot be formulated in thought, it will help at this stage to first inquire: what exactly do we mean by a thought? Thinking, at its most general, can perhaps take various forms. Indeed many, perhaps all, kinds of mental activity may be described as thinking. For example, to Descartes and Hume it was the occurrence of an idea, which was something like having a picture or image in the mind. However, by *thoughts* we shall mean here something quite specific; nowadays we understand that a mental image, such as a cow grazing, need not express a thought, and equally a thought need not be expressible as a pictorial image. Rather, when speaking of the limits of all possible thought, it is the *logical form* of these thoughts we shall be concerned with, and not pictorial images.

The thought that a particular cow is grazing is a mental

episode in which certain objects (cow, grass) are being mentally affirmed as being in a particular relation (grazing) to each other, whether depicted pictorially or not. In modern logic, this is an example of the simplest kind of thought. Here, the relation is a general term or *concept* which can be true of any number of objects, and for any such object it must be conceivable for the concept to be true, and equally conceivable for the concept to be false of that object. During any thought, one or more concepts are being ascribed by the mind to (conceived as true of) one or more particular objects. In the formal study of logic the thought that the cow is grazing on the grass could be represented by the formula *Grazing(cow, grass)*; other examples might be *Green(grass)*, *Taller-than(John, Mary)*. This formalism has the advantage that it allows the representation of abstract thoughts for which there may be no image, such as *Capital-city(Rome, Italy)*, *Overdrawn(Bank A/C 59047)*. A thought is then said to be true if the objects referred to by the thought are in the relation ascribed to them by its concept, and false if they are not in that relation.

From thoughts expressed as above, ascribing a single concept or relation to a single set of objects, the logical forms of more complex thoughts can be systematically built. For example, if *p, q* are any two thoughts, then the combined thought, *p and q* is true only if both *p, q* are true, otherwise it is false. Also, *not-p* is said to be true if and only if *p* is false. By such means as this (called 'truth-functions') complex thoughts like: 'None of the grass on which the cows are grazing is green' or 'It is possible to have several overdrawn bank accounts' etc. can be represented. Emotions and feelings might seem to be very different from this, but the reason Descartes wanted to describe most mental experiences also as thoughts is because when I am pleased, annoyed, hopeful or jealous there is normally some state of affairs, described by a thought, that I am pleased, annoyed or hopeful about, or somebody of whom I am jealous. Thus, most mental experiences are grounded in real or imagined events, i.e.

thoughts about the world.

Now to the Cartesian, and to the modern scientific temperament, the only way anything can be known or under-stood is by means of such conceptual thought, i.e. incorporating one or more objects under some general term that refers only to some objects and not to others. The only kind of intelligible mental content is held to be such thoughts: whatever is under-stood is a clear thought and whatever cannot be understood must be confused or unclear thoughts. This of course leaves no room for the possibility of intuitions which are not thoughts at all (they do not ascribe concepts to objects), but which may nevertheless be definite experiences guiding us to make precise choices.

I believe this can explain the kind of 'unhappy predicament' expressed by Viv Mitchell (in the passage cited in Chapter 3), for what is needed for her to grasp the timeless moment, or for the Unnameable to grasp the real silence, is to find some way of understanding apart from ascribing concepts to objects. That this is the true nature of the predicament is revealed when we consider what Mitchell says about 'concentrating on the here and now'. For what is concentrating? Surely it means preparing for thought or perception, preparing to conform all one's current mental experience to the concepts of here and of now. This means at each moment attending literally to here rather than to other places, and attending literally to now rather than to the past or the future. And this cannot be done without employing here and now as *concepts* excluding e.g. the past and the future; for concepts always exclude something.

However, what is needed for spirituality is to simply become self-aware, which is a mental state that does not exclude awareness of anything. Thus this must be a form of under-standing that *does not employ conceptual thought at all*. If spiritu-ality is indeed experienced non-conceptually as *timeless* then, paradoxically, the 'here and now' must also embrace the past and future as well as the present, not excluding any time. Only via this non-conceptual mental state do I 'step into the universal flow' for the latter does not describe any thinkable process, but is intended to trigger a different mode of understanding than thought altogether. It is precisely a requirement to surrender what we cling to as our very criterion (thought) of *whether we understand something*, which enables the bliss to be experienced – by allowing ourself to understand in a totally new way. Thus, it is not 'thinking too much' that causes the block to the higher Self 'we hear and read so much about'; it is thinking at the wrong moment, i.e. thinking at the precise moment when we should be abdicating from thought.

Furthermore, it is this assumption that there is no wrong moment, i.e. that *all* knowledge and understanding must be conceptual, which makes the spiritual experience seem so intellectually subtle and 'elusive'. For it is the conviction that if spirituality is intelligible at all, it can only be via concepts, and so if I fail to grasp spirituality, it must be too elusive for those concepts which I possess, and so perhaps I need more subtle concepts. Alternatively, one may resort, like the sceptics, to denying any meaning to spirituality since it is not expressible at all by concepts, and so any such 'understanding' is an illusion; this of course is a conclusion that is also frequently reached. But both responses rely upon assuming that meaning is synonymous with conceptual thought: in the one case the thoughts are too subtle to be understood; in the other case, there are no such thoughts to understand. It is the latter that is actually correct, but this need not be fatal to all meaning, since perhaps thought need not always be necessary for understanding. Recall from Chapter 2 the understanding needed by physical activities such as swordplay, scything, and even car repairs or teaching ability; here, success was apparently only attainable by employing means additional or alternative to thought, for it seemed, in these cases, that actions and responses needed to result from acting naturally, and thought was found to be sometimes detrimental to this. The question now arises as to whether something similar may be true in the purely contemplative sphere.

In these physical cases, it does seem that no academic study can provide the right kind of knowledge, since academic knowledge is confined solely to facts expressible in thought, i.e. the ascription of concepts to objects. Likewise, it seems that no human science can provide us with self-knowledge, because all the modern sciences and studies of man originated with the Cartesian method. In confining themselves purely to attempting to define man in thought, scientific knowledge only ever ascribes various concepts to him. Consequently, the Cartesian method cannot yield any non-conceptual truth about man and, equally, no human or social science can do so either. This is unsurprising if, whenever we do try to express any of this knowledge, we necessarily become mired in contradiction; for every academic discipline is committed above all else to logical consistency. And yet as we saw in the Kena Upanishad as well as in Zen Buddhism, logical contradiction was seen as unavoidable, and as almost a prerequisite for conveying the nature of the self-awareness experienced in meditation.

Nevertheless, this Eastern view of man must surely be in some sense the right one, since I can know any number of academic facts about myself without knowing the first thing about who I am, without being self-aware. This is a situation mercilessly parodied by the various works of Samuel Beckett, with their endless litanies of academic and other facts, leading nowhere. A few centuries earlier, another Irishman, Jonathan Swift, had, with his tale of Lemuel Gulliver, bitingly satirized how the majestic mind of man is cruelly 'tied down' by the Lilliputian demands of the sciences. This bondage is surely an image comparable to the poverty of the tramp at the information desk (Fig. 1). If we take these insights at all seriously, consider briefly the consequence. If ignorance of ourselves brings a kind of suffering, and it does, then this suffering cannot be cured by any kind of psychotherapy based upon scientific knowledge such as psychology or medicine. Nor can it be cured by quasi-scientific theories, like those of Freud or Jung. For by diagnosing and treating the problem only by means of conceptual knowledge, these disciplines all perpetuate the very disease they were designed to cure, namely our subservience to concepts. Rather, the only effective therapy must surely be, as the Buddha believed, by a different, non-conceptual kind of knowledge entirely. It is precisely this that is being proposed by the major religions, in the form of redemption, or enlightenment. Thus, it almost seems to be the very commitment to logical consistency itself that prevents the sciences providing us with the most vital information we need in life, namely: who are we, and where are we going?

On contradictions

We seem to be arriving at a conclusion that is extremely unpalatable to Western tastes, namely: a need to attach some kind of meaning to logical inconsistency, i.e. to contradictions. It is time we precisely defined therefore what we mean by a contra-diction. If *tall(John)* is a thought then we can represent the denial or negation of this thought by *not-tall(John)*. Now, by a contra-diction we mean a pair of conflicting thoughts, one of which is the negation of the other, and so they can never both be literally true. This would be the case for instance for the thoughts: *tall(John)*, *not-tall(John)*. We can see from this that the reason the statements contradict is because they have the logical form:

p, not-p

It follows that a pair of expressions of this form will always contradict, no matter what thought is being represented by *p*. This therefore is the general logical form of a contradiction. In other words, the inconsistency of thoughts is always due purely to their jointly possessing or entailing the above logical form, regardless of their content. For contradiction is always due to a thought being affirmed and denied at the same time, irrespective of what it is that is being affirmed or denied.

Let us now ask ourselves: can the pair of thoughts *p, not-p* ever express a clear and distinct idea? No, for on the one hand if *p* is a clear idea then so is *not-p*; in this case they cannot be combined into a single idea, but surely express a state of doubt or mental conflict in which no clear idea prevails. On the other hand, if *p* itself is an unclear idea, then so equally is *not-p*, and the result will tend to be not conflict but confusion; for here we might say that *p, not-p* can still combine to form an idea, albeit a confused one. E.g. the thought: 'James bought a cottage, but he can't afford the rent' appears to state that James both owns and does not own the cottage, and indicates confusion in the mind of the thinker, perhaps between the ideas of mortgage and rental. Also, for Descartes, as the thoughts become less clear, so too must the thinker's knowledge of her own existence, which is granted only by her thoughts, equally become less clear.

However, we also encountered a different view of contradiction. Regarding the Kena Upanishad in Chapter 3, we surmised that in the silence of meditation we might understand a kind of meaning other than thought. This held out at least the prospect of understanding *That which is not comprehended by the mind but by which the mind comprehends – know that to be Brahman.* For, recall that when we supposed this to be comprehended by the mind, it generated the contradiction that The Self both is and is not comprehended by the mind. From this we then concluded that the sentence must be comprehended by some means other than the mind, perhaps by intuition. Consequently, we did not feel pure confusion at this apparent contradiction of the kind described above, but rather we felt that we understood it in some new way. For if we did understand it, then it certainly was not by any thought in the mind at all, since then a contradiction is obtained, and no single coherent thought is ever expressed by a contradiction. This Kena example is of course further complicated by the fact that this is not just any contradiction; rather the subject matter of this particular contradiction is the very same as the subject matter of the Cogito itself, viz the limits of thought and the nature of the self.

To the Cartesian sceptic, there is no such intuitive alternative to thought by which Kena can be comprehended, and so the Kena text would simply be a contradiction. But this conclusion is really due to a *huge assumption being made by the Cartesians themselves,* viz: that whatever is not comprehended by thought as a clear and distinct idea has no meaning. Hence, thoughts which seem to contradict cannot ever express any other kind of knowledge, since there is no other kind of knowledge. However, this assumption was itself never proved, but was simply adopted by Descartes as axiomatic to his method. If we drop this assumption, then the apparent contradiction alone might no longer suffice (q.v. Chapter 3) to eliminate the meaning of Brahman since, despite not expressing a clear and distinct idea, this contradiction might nevertheless be said to have meaning of a different kind.

For we are exploring the possibility that there might be other precise ways to understand situations, apart from thought, which whenever we try to express them in thought invariably result in contradictions. If this is so, then in these special cases, if they exist, it might be better to characterize the acceptance of contradiction, not as manifesting confusion, but as the exact opposite, namely as *expressing a deep insight beyond thought.* In addition to Kena, Buddhism too, in the same vein, endorses a form of understanding, Enlightenment, that goes beyond thought, and which is only expressible by contradictions. Moreover, we noted how in medieval Europe St Teresa also tried to distinguish spiritual comprehending from conceptual understanding, and how Eckhart and others accepted knowledge of the soul via a kind of dark understanding or 'cloud of unknowing' which was never-theless tacitly recognized as a special kind of knowing not involving thought, and as by no means confused.

However, according to Descartes and the Unnameable there is a more draconian outlook; for when we contradict ourself we are not thinking clearly, and when we are not thinking clearly we cannot know anything at all. Hence *we cannot know we exist*, and so the Silence is out of reach; there is only the absence of thought, the existential Void, entailing oblivion. It seems therefore that what distinguishes the frightening Void from the reassuring Silence is the unintelligibility foisted upon it by the Cartesian assumption, namely: that it is only clear and distinct ideas (thoughts) that can ever be known or understood. This effec-tively prevents the void yielding any knowledge of one's existence. It is this Cartesian assumption that, for example, treats the positive experience of pure consciousness negatively, simply as an absence of thought, consequently denying it any meaning.

But now suppose there existed some way of *understanding* an absence of thought positively, as meaningful in its own right, and not merely as a negation, a lack, of that which provides meaning. In that case I might still, for example, understand myself to exist, even if I am not thinking, and the meaningless Void might thereby transform into a meaningful Silence. What kind of understanding could this possibly be? As a matter of fact, we know that pure consciousness, logically prior to thought, does enable us to know we exist, and to know we exist is surely, in some sense, to *understand* ourself to exist. So simple consciousness must itself be a form of understanding, and if there were an analysis explaining how we can understand in the absence of thought, then this should also contribute to explaining pure consciousness itself.

Chapter 5

The Turning Point

We seem to be confronted with a paradoxical task: to attempt to justify in thought how there can be a kind of comprehending other than thought. This means finding thoughts which can in some way characterize how such a particular experience of comprehending operates, without attempting to replace it by those thoughts. We have in fact seen examples of this when explaining our grasp of physical activities, which was shown to be not merely rhythmic or reflex, but inventive, whilst being at the same time non-conceptual. But can we identify something similar, purely in the realm of conceptual thought itself?

It may first help to start with a brief joke.

The other day, I staggered into my doctor's surgery and I said to him,
'Doctor, you've got to help me; I'm in a desperate state, I've just broken my
leg – in five *different places!'*
The doctor looked me up and down, and then he said:
'Well, if I were you, I wouldn't go to those places.'

I am indebted for this joke to the late, great Tommy Cooper.

Such levity may seem inappropriate to the seriousness of our quest for meaning in life, and yet I shall proceed to show how humour can nevertheless act as an effective fulcrum upon which to lever much weightier matters. The first thing I should like you to notice is that if we do laugh at this joke it is because we *understand* the joke. But my second point is to ask: does this understanding actually consist of thinking any thought? Now you will immediately point out there are lots of thoughts involved: thoughts about the doctor, thoughts about the patient, thoughts about his leg and so forth. My reply is that all these thoughts are necessary for the telling of the joke, but are they sufficient for understanding the joke? After all, it is perfectly possible to understand all the thoughts expressed in telling the joke, and still not understand the joke.

For the point which I want to convey is that at the precise moment when we understand the joke no thinking takes place, yet we laugh. To recap: by thinking, we mean ascribing some concept to one or more particular objects; thus to think the patient staggers is to ascribe the concept 'staggers' to the patient, and to think his leg is broken is to ascribe the concept 'broken' to his leg. But at the moment when we are grasping the joke there is no concept that we are ascribing to any object; and so, the grasping of the joke is not a thought. Evidence for this is the impossibility of fully explaining a joke to anyone. Explaining a joke is no laughing matter; the explanation is only ever a series of thoughts, and yet the humour is never merely the content of these thoughts but is always something more. Even if one manages to partially explain a joke to someone, the meaning of the joke is never given simply by thinking through the explanation, but always has to be another response added by oneself.

Thus, instead of being an obscure or esoteric matter, we find, on the contrary, that understanding without thinking is a familiar part of everyday life, namely whenever we find something funny. Our task now will be, of course, to explore the philosophical implications of this. For example, one thing should be immediately clear: that when understanding a joke we are certainly aware of existing, for we know it is *we* who are laughing. Thus Descartes was simply wrong that 'in order to exist, one must think'. While the context is wildly different, and it may seem irreverent, could this nevertheless provide a clue to the kind of mystical comprehending we were seeking for St Teresa, Meister Eckhart and the cloud of unknowing?

Notice that although the humour is not a thought, neither is it a complete blank, rather it has a content dependent on *other* thoughts, viz the thoughts in the joke. By examining these associated thoughts, we may be able to shed some light on the meaning of the joke itself, on how the joke actually is understood. So let us now examine more closely how we respond to the above joke.

First of all it may be questioned whether there is such a thing as the meaning of a joke; for, it may be said, all we can really identify is a feeling of surprise, or the fact that we laugh. So then the humour of the joke is not a meaning as such, but just an emotional or physical response to a stimulus, like sneezing. To this there is a very simple reply: since there is no difference between the surprise we feel at one joke from the surprise we feel at another joke, or the way we laugh at one joke from the way we laugh at another joke, if humour were just surprise or laughter then the humour of one joke would be indistinguishable from the humour of others, and all jokes would have the same meaning. But surely we do distinguish the meanings of different jokes, if only because the same person may understand one joke but not another. In any case, it is not strictly necessary to laugh at a joke or even be surprised by it in order to understand it. Consider for example a jaded producer of sitcoms: she may be able to understand a joke in a comedy script without herself finding it funny or eliciting any larger physical or emotional response.

So let us assume the above joke has a meaning, and let us set about establishing what it might be, given that it is not any of the thoughts expressed in the telling of the joke. The humour clearly seems to depend upon a misunderstanding between doctor and patient based upon their differing interpretations of the same sentence: 'I've just broken my leg – in *five* different places.' In short, part of the humour of the joke depends upon recognizing ambiguity, specifically concerning the word 'places': we must grasp both the patient's meaning of places on his leg, and also the doctor's meaning of places the leg can visit. So during the course of such a joke, we must suddenly switch our interpretation of a particular word, phrase or sentence from one meaning to another.

However, in the current example, the switch is not entirely unprovoked, but is necessitated by the need to make sense of the doctor's reply. We find we can't do this using the patient's interpretation of 'places' as positions on his leg, because it is of course impossible for a position on his leg to also be a venue visited by his leg. We see therefore that our need to reinterpret the word 'places' was driven by a clash or contradiction between the two possible meanings, and might not have been necessary otherwise. Indeed, if the two meanings had been consistent there may have been no humour at all. But in this case, unless we do alter our initial interpretation of 'places', the doctor's reply becomes unintelligible or nonsensical. And so at this point we experience momentary confusion or tension; but this is instantly relieved when we discover a second meaning for the same sentence. It is primarily this discovery, surely, that provides the relief when we laugh, and a sense of understanding, which resolves the confusion. We might then say that the humour consists in the pleasure at eliminating a contradiction produced by mistakenly interpreting a word in only one way, and which was successfully resolved by interpreting the word in two different ways.

But at no time during this process of confusion and its relief, I want to suggest, need any *thinking* be taking place; for thinking consists of interpreting symbols unambiguously, i.e. in only one way. Rather, the situation resembles more the example of visual recognition presented in Fig. 2. Here the interpretation of the diagram seems to switch between a vase (or chalice) and a pair of human faces, and back again spontaneously. But is there any thought taking place? No, in the case of visual recognition it seems clear that flipping between different meanings of the diagram is purely visual – we simply *recognize* the two meanings.

Now, let us focus upon one particular spot in the diagram.

This spot may be viewed as an uninterpreted sign, having two possible interpretations: firstly as perhaps a spot on someone's nose, secondly as a spot on a vase or chalice. But whichever it is, it cannot be both: a spot on someone's nose cannot be a spot on a vase, because a human face is not a vase. So there is a clash between these two interpretations, which is why we can only flip between the interpretations, but not experience them both at the same time. In the same way, I have been suggesting that the two interpretations of the uninterpreted sign 'places' are experienced as incompatible and so cannot be held at the same time. However, a text expresses a single clear thought only if it can be interpreted in just one way, i.e. it lacks ambiguity. Hence the above joke, being ambiguous, cannot adequately be understood by just a single thought. Rather, the understanding of the 'higher' meaning of the joke consists in flipping between the different interpretations of the same sign, without the intervention of any thoughts. This then provides an example of what we were seeking: a mode of understanding other than thought.

It is only if we are forced to keep the same interpretation of a word like 'places' throughout, as in a scientific or logical text, that the narrative of the joke becomes meaningless, and a person who endeavours to grasp the above joke in this way would invariably fail, and would normally be said to lack a sense of humour. Notice the similarity here, with our inference from the Kena Upanishad, that any attempt to express the intuition of Brahman in terms of conceptual thought is, because of its inexpressibility, bound to result in self-contradiction, i.e. nonsense, and so is doomed to failure. Perhaps the inexpressibility of humour is an example of the same thing.

Indeed, it may be fruitful to apply Happold's list of the typical characteristics of mystical experience cited in Chapter 2 to see if humour might qualify as a mystical experience. We immediately notice the two characteristics which I added to the list, namely *freedom* and also *joy*. For the very purpose of humour is an explosion of joy, and we undeniably feel free at that moment, perhaps liberated from the contradiction or confusion a moment earlier. But now, if we go through Happold's list in order, we also find that since the meaning of a joke can never be fully explained, it is always (1) *ineffable*, but at the same time, as we have just noted, we nevertheless understand the joke, and so obviously there is (2) a *noetic* quality to the experience. Although the telling of a joke may well be long and rambling, the actual moment of 'seeing' the joke is normally only a flash of understanding and is not prolonged, thus resembling the *transiency* (3) of much reported mystical experience. And when we grasp a joke, don't we normally feel we have been given something, a free gift, which was not a result of our own devising? In that case it fulfils the *passivity* condition (4) for the mystical.

It is interesting that, in the joke we just examined, the humour succeeded in uniting conflicting interpretations by the doctor and the patient. This sense of release at finding unity in diversity is surely a *consciousness of oneness*, which is number (5) on our list. It certainly constitutes a harmony of opposites in some sense. In laughing at a joke do we also experience a sense (6) of *timelessness*? It seems to me that we do: although the joke itself may describe various events occurring in time, at the moment of humour we are 'taken out of ourself' not noticing our surroundings. Without intending any disrespect, surely we might even compare this with the kind of timeless moment reported by saints and visionaries, and described by TS Eliot (Chapter 2). Finally of course, we are always aware that it is *we* who understand the joke, and despite not thinking at that moment, we are fully aware of existing. Yet we are passive, so the *self* (7) of whom we are mystically aware at this time is not the 'strong, self-conscious feeling of 'I', but may be No-I, our higher self, making itself known independent of thought. In the light of these considerations, it does seem that the flash of humorous understanding (which I shall in future refer to as an *aha* moment) may be mystical in nature.

I want to now consider a subtle objection by a sceptic, to the effect that my analysis is incorrect and that, while humour is indeed a form of understanding, it is an understanding that can be adequately characterized by thought, and there is nothing mystical about it. To facilitate the argument, I present it in the form of a dialogue:

SCEPTIC: The understanding of the joke that you have just described is misleading, since it still consists in having a thought, namely the thought that the word 'places' has changed its interpretation from one kind of thing to another.

JOKER: No, the word is certainly being interpreted differently, I grant, but that does not mean we are having the *thought* that we are interpreting the word differently.

S: But since all understanding is thought, that is nevertheless what we *must* be doing. We must just be having the thought at high speed, too fast for us to notice, or else thinking the thought unconsciously, or both.

J: Well, that might sound plausible, but I shall now demonstrate that your hypothesis is not possible: we may well be aware of switching our interpretation of the word 'places', but we have no *thought* that we are doing this. For, the meaning of the joke *does not consist in any thought at all*, not even the thought that the interpretation of a particular word or sentence has changed. And indeed, I should like to say that when we laugh, no such thought is ever the object of our mirth, not even unconsciously.

S: That sounds intriguing. Why ever not?

J: Well, as we both agree, the humour of the above joke is due to understanding in some way how one interpretation of a word is replaced by another.

S: Yes, and I claim this is simply a thought process in which we consider how making a distinction between the doctor's meaning and the patient's meaning can eliminate the apparent contradiction that a place on my leg is also said to be a place my leg can visit.

J: But surely, in grasping the joke, we were doing more than that, we were reacting to the apparent contradiction itself, and not merely thinking about it.

S: Certainly, but that is just our behaviour; it is not understanding.

J: No, I mean that the way we actually understand the joke is, by the very act of splitting our own interpretation of 'places' in two, in response to the conflict. Thus in this case, the experience of understanding consists in splitting a meaning; and this is not the thinking of any thought. It is this that provides the release from the confusion of thinking a place on my leg can also be a place my leg can visit, and it is surely the distinguishing of these interpretations that is *the act of understanding itself*. So my understanding of the joke is not just to think thoughts about these different interpretations, simply on the assumption that thinking is the only way to understand anything. Rather, I engage in a different kind of understanding altogether: *understanding an apparent contradiction*. And this consists in the mind not simply thinking about meaning-changes, but actually executing those changes itself.

S: I see your point. But even if I do concede that this mental activity is a form of understanding then it would evidently be a strange form of understanding. In fact I'm not clear why we are entitled to think of such mental gymnastics as understanding at all.

J: The reason surely is because we do indeed call seeing the humour of a joke: 'understanding' that joke – so, if splitting the various meanings of a word or phrase in response to an apparent contradiction is appreciating the humour, then such a dynamic process is also the understanding itself. Furthermore, this also proves that your own theory must be wrong.

S: How so?

J: Well, do you agree that for any sentence to express a thought, it must, by contrast, apparently be logically consistent, and not a contradiction?

S: Of course.

J: Now, consider the thought which you propose as giving the meaning of the joke: must it be consistent or inconsistent?

S: Since it expresses a coherent thought, any such meaning for the joke must of course be logically consistent.

J: But I believe you have also provisionally accepted that the humour of the joke requires us to initially experience a contradiction – contrary to our purely thinking a logically consistent thought. What therefore must be our conclusion?

S: Reluctantly, I have to admit that no thought about a joke can ever provide our understanding of the joke, because to grasp the joke we have to initially contradict ourself, which is the opposite of thinking a logically consistent thought.

J: Exactly. And doesn't this account for the familiar fact that the explanation of a joke is always singularly unfunny? It is because, in understanding a joke, we are always reacting to a contradiction, but in understanding an explanation we never are.

It seems, therefore, that the mental process of understanding this joke is not purely a process of thought. Rather, it seems to just be the discovery of a new interpretation for some occurrences of a word, which is prompted by an apparent contradiction that resulted from using only the old interpretation. This may be quickly followed by a process of mentally flipping between the two interpretations. It is by performing these mental acts, not by thinking thoughts about ambiguity, that we understand the ambiguity of the joke.

The English humourist and logician Lewis Carroll made a not unrelated point about logical inference itself, for he pointed out that understanding the logical inference of a thought q from another thought p did not consist in thinking any further thought

r. He portrayed this amusingly, as follows. In a philosophical dialogue called *What the Tortoise said to Achilles* (1895), Carroll considers what is the nature of inferring a conclusion Z from premises A, B. He proposes through Achilles that this amounts merely to thinking the thought: 'If A and B are true, Z must be true.' However, while the tortoise believes this thought as well as A, B, he stubbornly refuses to infer the conclusion, Z, thereby demonstrating to us that he does not understand the nature of inference after all. When the tortoise asks, innocently, what would be the consequence of his not accepting Z, Achilles replies in exasperation:

> Then Logic would take you by the throat and force you to do it!... Logic would tell you, 'You can't help yourself. Now that you've accepted A and B, you must accept Z!' so you've no choice, you see.

But of course he does have a choice; or rather, he has as much or as little choice as a person to laugh at a joke, since in each case it is a natural property of the mind to make these transitions. The moral of the story is that our understanding that the truth of q logically follows from the truth of p is not given by any thought r, but is simply an ability, a skill, at reaching true consequences q from true premises p. The tortoise understands a description of this skill, but appears to lack the skill himself.

Instead of applying humour to the nature of logic, let us now apply logic to the nature of humour. Apart from being an amusing way of doing logic, what is the relevance of *Achilles and the Tortoise* to the nature of humour itself? The answer is that we may see from it that understanding humour bears a relationship to understanding logical reasoning. This is because both are movements of the mind associated with various thoughts, but without actually being thoughts.

There is a stronger kinship, however, for one may be viewed as the opposite of the other. From one interpretation of 'places' in our earlier joke, recall that we arrived at a factually incompatible interpretation of 'places'. We know of course that humour can be crazy, madcap or anarchic and so we expect it to be illogical in a general sense. But it can also be regarded as anti-logical in a more technical sense, for each pursues the opposite of the other. A joke is a special kind of narrative or text which, unlike normal prose, is actually *intended* to be logically inconsistent, and recognized as such, whereas literal prose is normally required to be self-consistent. For a joke is understood, not as prose, but by finding a second interpretation for a word, phrase or sentence, which enables the text to clearly present two different meanings. From the initial interpretation of 'places' as positions on my leg, the joke suddenly seemed to require 'places' to also mean places my leg can visit. This ability to devise such new meanings, contrary to the assumed meaning of a text, seems to be an essential part of our ability to understand jokes.

Both logic and humour therefore clearly reveal the human ability to recognize when thoughts are or are not consistent with one another. Carroll showed that the logical ability to deduce true consequences of true assumptions is not merely the ability to think a particular thought. Conversely, we have now also seen that the humorous ability to recognize certain *false* consequences of our 'true' assumptions was likewise not the ability to think any particular thought. In our example, initially accepting as true the doctor's interpretation logically implied rejecting as false the patient's interpretation, and vice versa. Like logic, humour is a movement of the mind that expresses a form of understanding, but whereas logic endeavours to avoid contradictions, humour seems to actively court contradictions.

When we try to apply two logically contrary interpretations of a word at once to the same object we experience the confusion of contradiction. By contrast, the doctor and patient each separately knows clearly what he means: while each admittedly misunderstands the other, they do not individually feel confused. In other words, it is when there is only one voice for both meanings that there can be confusion and contradiction; I call this the *univocal* interpretation, normal for scientific or logical prose, but unsuitable for a joke. However, with a *bivocal* narrative, or dialogue, the narrative is interpreted by two or more voices (e.g. Patient/Doctor) in which each of the conflicting interpretations can be assigned to a different voice, thereby averting the threatened contradiction. This is exactly the sense of relief we experience when understanding the meaning of a joke. The contradiction is due to initially interpreting the joke univocally, like ordinary prose, but the relief of the laughter is only attained by then reinterpreting it bivocally, i.e. by realizing some tokens of a word (by the patient) are to be interpreted one way, and other tokens (by the doctor) to be interpreted another way.

Instead of explicitly mentioning two human speakers, a bivocal text may take univocal form, simply requiring within the given text that there be two different modes of interpreting different tokens (occurrences) of the same words, phrases or sentences. Indeed, such a text is what would ordinarily be called ambiguous. We can now clarify what we mean by a concept in such cases: it is a particular interpretation of a word or phrase. Thus one interpretation of a word (like 'places') would signify one concept, and another interpretation of the same word would signify another concept. In this way, entirely different concepts can be linked by the same sign. A thought is of course the ascription of a concept or concepts to an object, so it can be expressed by the ascription of interpreted words or phrases to an object. Confusion can result when two tokens of the same word are intended to be interpreted differently, but are mistakenly interpreted in the same way; i.e. the ambiguity is not noticed.

It is, however, only intended expressions of thought that are subject to the laws of logic, i.e. words whose tokens are interpreted in only one way (univocally), and which lack ambiguity. The fact, however, that we can nevertheless understand ambiguity shows that there is a form of understanding other than logical thought, and that there is an activity of understanding other than the activity of thinking. More precisely: there is a form of understanding a text other than understanding it univocally, viz: by perceiving its ambiguity, such understanding may be termed anti-logical since construed unambiguously it often leads to contradiction.

The moment we try to substitute conceptual thought, of whatever degree of sophistication, for what we understand when we understand jokes, we misrepresent the humour of the joke. Hence there can never be an adequate theory of jokes. For suppose some such theory of a joke were true; then the moment we come to think the theory, the joke ceases to be funny, so the theory did not define the meaning of the joke after all.[1] The underlying reason for this observation is to do with the fact that every theory relies on conceptual thought. The meaning of the joke is its humour and it seems that the humour never consists of conceptual thought because conceptual thought is subject to the laws of logic, whereas humour actively pursues contradiction in the form of ambiguity, incongruity, or absurdity. It does this by initially assuming logic, i.e. by making us naïvely assume that different occurrences of the same symbol or word must always have the same interpretation, and trapping us in a contradiction. However, the very essence of much humour then consists in the mental activity of finding different interpretations for the same word, thereby releasing us from the contradiction. This is something the mind can do with the meanings of its words, but which no consistent theory can do with the meanings of its sentences; no theory can reinterpret itself. That is the main reason why all theories are intrinsically humourless.

At this point it might plausibly be posited that what I have just done is to myself develop a *theory of jokes* 'of some degree of sophistication' that consists entirely of conceptual thought. So aren't I contradicting myself in denying the possibility of such a theory? My reply is that a theory about *how* we understand jokes in general is very different from a theory of *what* we understand when we understand a particular joke. Part of understanding the joke itself is often to solve a contradiction by creating two conflicting interpretations of the same word, phrase or sentence in our head at the same time, e.g. the two interpretations of 'places' in the above example. This is a particular kind of mental activity, and, as we have seen, no theory can define it completely since otherwise the theory itself would generate this activity, i.e. it would be self-contradictory – and hence not a consistent theory. But now distinguish this from the mental activity involved in understanding, not the joke, but the process of understanding the joke. By this I mean understanding this general *requirement* to eliminate an apparent contradiction by creating two different interpretations in the mind at the same time. Then this latter mental activity consists in nothing more than conceptual thought, viz: thinking about the possibility of two such interpretations and what the mind needs to do with them. For in *describing* our use of the two interpretations in this way, every word retains the same meaning throughout the narrative; at no point does the same word have to be comprehended with two different meanings during the explanation (and it is for this reason of course that the explanation is not funny). Rather the opposite, all ambiguity must be eliminated if clarity is to be achieved. And this is the way language normally operates.[2]

However, understanding language in this conventional way to explain the mental activities of humour is very different from understanding a text humorously by altering one's own interpretation of its words. Like riding a bicycle, analysing how you do something is very different from actually doing it. The former is always conceptual thought and the latter is normally a form of understanding other than thought. What makes the current case so much more confusing than riding a bicycle is that the accomplishment expresses not a physical skill but a mental one – thus resembling the skill used in subsequently analysing it. Instead of physical movements, this skill of laughter manipulates thoughts, the very kinds of intellectual element used in its own explanation. And since no theory can explain the humour of a joke without becoming humourless, I conclude that a theory of what people do to understand jokes is possible, but a theory of the meanings of jokes is not possible. And we know this, even before we begin to propose any theories at all. The madcap world of comedy with its offbeat slant on life seems with its pursuit of contradictions to be proposing, not so much an alternative world (for the laws of logic hold good for all possible worlds, no matter how weird) as no world at all. I venture to suggest that previous theories of humour have failed (e.g. Freud's) for precisely that reason – they have tried to give a *theory*; whereas the only theory that is possible is a theory that shows why no theory is possible.

As far as the above joke is concerned, there is in any case probably more to its humour than the simple wordplay I have identified. The doctor/patient exchange is particularly innocent, lacking all satire, irony, symbolism, political allusions and so forth. Nevertheless, other factors in the humour do exist, for example the unsympathetic doctor seems almost to reprove the patient for frequenting the kind of places where one's leg is liable to get broken. This is an incongruous suggestion, and 'contradicts' both the professionalism and the compassion we normally expect from a doctor. The result is to add to the joke another layer of ambiguity, at a purely psychological, i.e. non-verbal, level.

However, my aim here was not in any case to produce a general theory of humour, or even of jokes, but rather the intensely serious one of endeavouring to identify a kind of understanding that might help resolve the dilemma of being human. The aim has been to seek a new way to explain the kind of experience that enlightenment might conceivably be. From the above brief account, we saw that no theory of humour can really be possible, and in future chapters it should become clear why, for similar reasons, the same must also be true for spiritual enlightenment concerning life as a whole.

Chapter 6

The Cognitive Value of Ambiguity

In order to consider how the special kind of understanding we exhibit in humour may be extended from mere entertainment to having cognitive and existential significance in our life, I should now like to make what may seem a strange suggestion: that humour and practical wisdom ('wit and wisdom') are alike. That we may understand serious aphorisms in a very similar way that we understand jokes, i.e. that the wisdom of aphorisms, epigrams and other wise sayings often resides in the fact that they contradict themselves. They do this not to extinguish meaning but to create new meaning. Far from being nonsense, these sayings are deeply meaningful because they are revelatory of one of the major poles of the human mind: the non-rational or intuitive. If they appear to violate the rules of language it is often only so as to create new language.

We might, for instance, like to think the word 'friend' embraces all kinds of friendship ranging from casual acquaintance to intimate love, and indeed the word is used with this degree of variation. But now consider this remark by Schopenhauer:

Everybody's friend is nobody's friend. — — — — —-(1)

The curious thing about this sentence is that it has the logical form of a contradiction and so it cannot in any obvious way express a thought, and indeed the statement may leave us initially confused. For on a literal interpretation this sentence is a flat contradiction and the perfectly rational man should not be able to understand it. However, most people, upon reflection, have no difficulty understanding what Schopenhauer meant by this sentence, except perhaps philosophers trained on principle to take every word literally. The interesting question therefore is: how do most ordinary people nevertheless manage to understand the sentence, and moreover see that it might even be true?

The key lies in the fact that some aspects of friendship may lead us to think one can be everybody's friend, and different aspects may lead us to deny this. However, it is a principle of logic and the linguistic expression of thought that it be univocal: i.e. that ambiguity is to be avoided and that different occurrences of the same symbol should always mean the same thing. E.g. for any name such as 'John' (signifying a particular object), the statement 'John is John' is a tautology and 'John is not John' is a contradiction. This could only be logically guaranteed if both occurrences of 'John' are compelled to refer to the same person. In the abstract form, $a=a$ is a law of logic known as the Principle of Identity, and is a way of stipulating that, as far as logic is concerned, both occurrences of a have to refer to the same thing. (For if the two as could refer to different things then it would not necessarily be true that $a=a$.) Now, in the example above, 'friend' is admittedly a general term signifying a concept, rather than a name, but it can be shown that a similar Principle of Identity also applies to general terms.[1] Thus, we can see that if we do understand the apparent contradiction (1) then we cannot be interpreting it in the way required by logic or language, but rather we are allowing the same word to have different meanings according to where it is in the sentence. But if 'friend' does take different meanings in different places, nothing about the outward form of the sentence tells us what these different meanings must be. There is thus no logical evidence from (1) that it is the paradoxical or unorthodox expression of a unique thought. So perhaps when we understand such a paradox we are not understanding it as a thought at all. To investigate this further, therefore, let us now consider some of the implications of friendship.

On the one hand it is perfectly possible to be universally popular, and thus be 'everybody's friend'. And if you are indeed a friend of everybody, then the conclusion that you are 'nobody's friend' will be untrue. On the other hand, we may also see that it is impossible to be everybody's friend. One reason we may think this is to believe there might simply not be enough hours in the day to be a friend of everybody. Another reason may be to view the whole of (1) as a logical inference: '*if* you are everybody's friend, *then* you are nobody's friend'. For, suppose Gil is everybody's friend, and consider some possible consequences: if two of these friends are competing for the same job or find themselves rivals for the same man, then which of them is Gil to help? To assist one is necessarily to oppose the other; so it seems she cannot be a friend to them both. Finally, since everyone is in competition with somebody, then, for each person, Gil's loyalty to that person cannot be relied upon. So Gil is nobody's friend. Perhaps Schopenhauer is simply saying it is for reasons like these that it is impossible to be a friend of everybody. We may view this depth of thought as logical depth; a depth fully disclosed by the logic of the situation. Such a form of argument is called in logic a *reductio ad absurdum*: from an assumption of universal friendship we deduce an absurdity (a contradiction), therefore the assumption was false.

But, in view of what we had previously believed about friendship, we should now be genuinely confused, because some people had manifestly seemed to us to be everybody's friend, yet it seems we have just proved this to be logically impossible. Interpreted as expressing a thought about all possible friends, therefore, Schopenhauer seems to be suggesting that our concept of friendship is confused and inconsistent. For it seems that it both is and is not possible to be everybody's friend. This hidden inconsistency is deliberately exploited in the formulation of the paradox (1). And yet somehow, we may not actually feel puzzled by this inconsistency, for a sudden insight (an aha moment) may make us feel not only that we understand the sentence, but that it is undeniably true. In that case, we must be understanding the self-contradictory remark by some means other than as the logical (univocal) expression of some thought.

It seems that the aha requires us to understand the statement in a new kind of way. It is surely the realization intuitively that 'friend' is being used in two different senses – but without it being revealed what these senses are. The logical form of a contradiction has, so to speak, opened up a fault line in the concept, along which it may fracture. By splitting the confused concept 'friend' into two consistent but not fully known concepts, say *friend-1, friend-2*, we gain the understanding that we may be able to extinguish the contradiction. And I submit that detecting, merely from the logical implications of friendship, the possible existence of such a pair of interpretations is primarily what constitutes the aha, in this case, allowing us to grasp a logical basis for:

Everybody's friend-1 is nobody's friend-2. — — — — —-(2)

It is only *after* such an intuition of *friend-1, friend-2* that they may be subsequently conceived and identified in thought.

For we may now say, for example, that somebody who is a casual friend to everybody is of course nobody's deep friend or, equally, assert some other dichotomy satisfying the logical form of (2). This means we now interpret the sentence (1) as ambiguous, and one that cannot be interpreted univocally at all. The paradox may now be completely removed by replacing (1) by the bivocal interpretation:

Everybody's casual friend is nobody's close friend. — — — — —-(3)

Some such interpretation of (1), breaking the principle of identity, may now be regarded as the final resolution of the paradox. However, what I should particularly like to emphasize is that these or other kinds of friendship that turn out to be pivotal in interpreting the paradox bivocally *may not be concepts we previously possess* and hence may not be available to the mind at the moment of understanding. Rather, they seem to be created or formed by the very process (2) of understanding itself. Actually, it was simply our need to comprehend the contradiction (1), forcing us to examine the various conflicting complex requirements of friendship, that enabled us first to detect and then to conceptualize *friend-1, friend-2*. In other words, the aha was a creative act of concept-formation. For it was the paradox itself that prompted us to think deeply about friendship, and this was surely Schopenhauer's intention. Our altered concepts were then formed only to avert the threatened contradiction, and we may not have succeeded in articulating them otherwise.

As with the joke, the paradox is resolved by a discovery of how to interpret the same word in two different ways. But unlike the joke, the aha is initially a recognition of something rather less specific. The first token of 'friend' is interpreted only as (something like) a casual friend, and the second token only as (something like) a close friend. But we can only flip between these two interpretations when they have crystallized into particular concepts. The contradiction provides extreme pressure, causing this binary fission to take place along the fault line provided by the logical form of a contradiction. We have resolved the contradiction by a cognitive advance, replacing a single confused interpretation of a word by two simpler clearer interpretations of the same word, which may not previously have been identified by us. In the process of this creative act, a self-contradictory concept has been replaced instead by a pair of consistent concepts that are contrary to each other, or mutually exclusive. This was due to the inspiration, or stress, induced by a 'friendly' contradiction that we nevertheless feel we understand, in other words, a paradox.

To summarize: initially we start off thinking there is just one kind of friendship, but the surprising fact that we understand from the contradiction educates us that there must really be two kinds of friendship – *friend-1, friend-2* – being named by the same word. Our consequent search for these concepts is due to the contradiction, since with a consistent sentence we would be perfectly content with the concepts we already have. And notice that *the understanding of the contradiction (assenting to it) comes first*, in a flash of insight, affirming the existence of future concepts *friend-1, friend-2*. Only after this do we grasp them as particular new concepts, in the consistent thought (3), thus finally resolving the contradiction. This means that the thought (3) is *not* the way we understand the contradiction (1). Rather, it was only as a result of understanding the intermediate stage (2), via anonymous *friend-1, friend-2*, that a thought such as (3) became possible. Thus when we initially saw the possible truth of (1), it was only on its own ambiguous terms, rather than by any concrete thought, or pair of thoughts.

What we understood, at that aha moment, was not our original concept 'friend' that had been found wanting, still less two replacement concepts such as 'real friend' or 'apparent friend' which resulted from this understanding. No, rather what we understood was not any concept at all, but simply the unfamiliar possibility of interpreting two occurrences of 'friend' differently, yet within the context of our previous understanding of friendship. And this is because we understood all at once the stresses and strains acting on any friendship, and how two opposing interpretations of *friend-1, friend-2* could separate some of the ways in which the existing concept was inconsistent and therefore unsatisfactory. All of this is what we call *understanding a contradiction*, a form of understanding clearly different from conceptual or logical thought, i.e. ascribing concepts to objects. The contradictory format of (1), in preventing us from under-standing its words as a thought, consequently prompted us to find some form of understanding other than thought; that is exactly what the flash of insight succeeded in doing for us.

I conclude that our intuitive understanding of the contradiction (1) is not any kind of thought; nor does it simply consist, as in the case of the joke, in the same word being used in two different senses – since these two senses were not already known. Rather, we classified an old word in two *new* ways; and it is very much in this sort of fashion that we constantly create new classifications for special purposes, out of old concepts, in our daily lives. In fact we may say we have *polarized* our original concept into opposing aspects of friendship. From the inconsistent concept of a friend, we have generated a pair of perfectly consistent concepts, of the kind Aristotle called *contraries* (e.g. close friend, casual friend), because they cannot both be true of an object at the same time.[2]

We saw that, in the case of humour, the realization that a word was being used in two contrary senses was the end of the matter – that was the whole point of the joke; but in the case of wisdom it is only the beginning. After contemplating the inconsistencies of friendship we see more clearly the difference between real bonds of friendship experienced from the inside, and popularity, the mere appearance of friendship, observable to others. As a result, we may now be led into new insights into human nature, meriting the title 'wisdom'. Unlike the crazy inconsistencies of the joke, which lead nowhere, the inconsistencies of the aphorism (1) are used to split an existing concept down the middle, a valuable and quite pragmatic result. We have in this way gained some philosophical illumination, which may genuinely help us in the practical friendships we may form, or perhaps fail to form, in our daily lives. Moreover, this practicality did not consist in verifying any generalized empirical thoughts about social relationships. Rather, it consisted in altering the very concepts by means of which we can think such thoughts, and hence judge such relationships. If true social thoughts constitute knowledge, then the insight provided by the apparent contradiction (1), modifying the very concepts by which we think these thoughts, might thereby qualify as 'wisdom', rather than knowledge.

For, even before I have finally formulated these new concepts (3) of friendship, the contradiction (1) is able to modify my understanding and treatment of other people. In other words, my obscure grasp of *friend-1, friend-2* enables me to partly act in the present *as if* I already had the concepts and thoughts I will only fully possess in the future. In this case, the apparent contradiction (1) has drawn my attention to some of the conflicts necessarily at play in friendship (perhaps causing me to beware of befriending every member of a small community, in which rivalries exist). These insights, this wisdom, do not though consist of conceptual thoughts, since they are only expressed by a contradiction, making thought impossible. Our wiser actions are, therefore, evidence for a *mode of understanding other than thought* which, unlike humour, can be of practical advantage.

Wise sayings

The mental activity we call wisdom seems not in general to consist of conceptual thought, for the latter is always the ascription of concepts to objects, and the logical consequences of these. These ascriptions and their consequences, if true, we call, not wisdom, but factual knowledge. Rather, wisdom is always the product of intuitions which seem to be 'anti-logical' in the sense that they are the result of interpreting contradictions, which then stimulate the mind to interpret old words in new ways. In order to further investigate these activities of intuition, let us now consider some more examples of wise sayings. Consider for instance the following:

a) *The clown is often the best acrobat.*

In his act, the clown falls and tumbles but the acrobat is always poised and graceful. So naïvely the acrobat is more skilful than the clown. Hence the above statement *a*) conflicts with this, initially producing a contradiction, which we should not be able to understand. However, an aha moment may nevertheless enable us to understand it, for the aha perceives that the pratfalls of the clown may not be all that they seem. Upon reflection, there may then be the further realization that, while not actually falling, it may be even more skilful to pretend to fall (clown) than not to fall at all (acrobat), for it requires not only the skill of the acrobat in not falling, but also the added skill of pretending to fall. Where then is the wisdom in this observation? It surely consists in the fact that these deeper insights into clowning are contrary to appearance, i.e. were evoked by a contradiction. In other words, the wise thoughts result from an aha process of coming to understand an apparent contradiction, by a means *other than thought*. The thoughts themselves are actually only possible after the aha has crystallized real from simulated falling, and real from apparent skill, as pairs of contrary concepts. This may then result in the possibly unfamiliar concept that ungainly acts can sometimes be more skilful than graceful ones.

Such wisdom may well be generalized to analogous circumstances further afield. In these cases, the resolution of the contradiction may instil in us a general grasp of how someone can simulate incompetence in one sphere (e.g. acrobatics) so as to attain achievement in an unrelated sphere (e.g. comedy). In this way, a detective, for example, may deliberately feign ignorance of certain facts so as to coax valuable testimony out of a witness or suspect.

Such a concept may entail a pattern of behaviour that is new to the observer, and unsuspected before grasping the above contradiction.

Now consider the wisdom of a proverb:

b) Don't lock the stable door after the horse has bolted.

We lock things away to prevent their loss. So to lock a stable door *after* the loss of the horse is to try to prevent from happening what has already happened, a manifest contradiction (by thinking of the horse as if it were still present). Where then is the wisdom? It consists in splitting the confused references to the horse into the two contraries: absent and present. For, only locking away a horse that is actually present will have any effect, not locking away an absent horse.

If the last example was a little mundane, the following quote from Oscar Wilde is more elevated:

c) *Punctuality is the thief of time.*

As with so many of Wilde's remarks, this reverses a Christian homily:

d) *Procrastination is the thief of time.*

This latter is easily understood, and not particularly wise; indeed it seems a truism or platitude. It is for this reason surely that Wilde's reversal of it seems to be a contradiction, for what could be a more efficient method of saving time than punctuality? We ought to be unable to understand this contradiction, and yet somehow, by an aha, we can. As before, the aha seems to intimate to us that time is being understood in two ways, *time-1, time-2* in the same thought; punctuality concerning *time-1* is the thief of *time-2*. Thus the sentence is deliberately ambiguous. The aha provides us with an *intuition* that there is another notion of time, which is 'stolen' whenever appointments are kept or trains arrive on time. What could this be?

Perhaps *time-2* is a kind of time that cannot be measured by clocks, and so cannot be rationed or apportioned according to a plan; procrastination would thus not be possible with *time-2*, neither would punctuality. Wilde seems to be saying there are better ways of spending time than keeping appointments. Perhaps by *time-2* we might mean uncommitted time or leisure that might be precious to us. Or, we might think, for example, of being absorbed in an activity, such as creating a work of art, which might be ruined by being interrupted for an appointment. For as TS Eliot said, the timeless moment nevertheless occurs in time, and is actually a way of using time, as are meditation and prayer, which would surely be interrupted or 'stolen' by punctuality. Would prayer count as procrastination? If so, then ironically we see that Wilde's apparently cynical rejoinder *c*) may actually be more spiritual than the original Christian injunction *d*).

Since we still have not finally decided which of these interpretations was indeed Wilde's intended meaning, this example amply demonstrates how we are able to intuit the *existence* of a pair of unknown contraries, *time-1, time-2*, simply by feeling we understand a particular contradiction, without yet crystallizing them into concrete concepts.

Perhaps it should be a source of concern that the kind of sentences we reject as illogical are precisely what many other cultures use as a vehicle to convey their deepest wisdom. Conversely, on other occasions, a statement that appears to us to have a straightforward logical meaning may be viewed by another tradition as being paradoxical. We see this, for example, from the Sufi mystics of Islam such as Saadi from Shiraz in Persia, who said:

e) No one throws stones at a barren tree.

This sentence is not a contradiction; rather the contradiction must be supplied by the reader. For, as with Western aphorisms this presents within the space of one short sentence two opposing special cases of a more general concept, namely misfortune. Firstly, a barren tree or person not producing any fruit may be viewed as unfortunate. But, in another sense, that person is fortunate because no one will covet what the person has or attack him for it since (like the Sufi) he has nothing. And so the same tree is both fortunate and unfortunate, an apparent contradiction. Here, our ability to distinguish the 'subtlety' of two kinds of fortune (*fortunate-1, fortunate-2*) arises directly as a result of a contradiction in an initial simplistic concept of a single overall fortune/misfortune.

Again Saadi also said:

f) The alchemist dies in pain and frustration – while the fool finds treasure in a ruin.

For Saadi, the treasure of the fool refers to the spiritual riches of the Sufi, while the alchemist symbolizes preoccupation with earthly riches. The fool thus both finds and fails to find treasure. From this contradiction we are led to suspect there may be two kinds of treasure: *treasure-1, treasure-2* and, correspondingly, two kinds of fool.

In China, Lao Tzu, the founder of Taoism, said (see Chapter 2):

g) Though clay be moulded into a vase, the utility of the vase lies in what is not there.

However, it must also be admitted that the clay of the vase is useful, since the space was there before the vase was created, and will remain after the vase is destroyed; but in neither of these cases is the space useful. And yet *g)* is also true: it is indeed the space which provides the 'utility of the vase'. And so the clay of the vase both does and does not provide the utility of the vase; an apparent contradiction. Here, however, the paradox is being used in a manner more complex than in the previous examples, having, I believe, an extra level of meaning.

Instead of being used to suggest two different meanings for

the utility of a vase, the paradox is being used primarily as a *metaphor* for the general 'utility' of paradox itself. For surely one possible interpretation of Lao Tzu's purpose in this utterance is that, although concepts may be moulded into a thought, the utility (meaning) of the thought lies in what is not conceived, i.e. that the ultimate nature of meaning (the Tao) is not itself conceivable by thought, but only by paradoxes such as this one. The utterance symbolizes all this by means of an apparent contradiction, in which the utility of the vase is interpreted ambiguously: not only as the clay of which it is made (thought), but also as the space (intuition) enclosed by the clay.

A practical example of wisdom

When encountering a contradiction, we are now in a position to distinguish the very real glimmerings of intuition from mere confusion, and thus drive a wedge between ideas (thoughts) that are clear and distinct on the one hand, and ideas that are obscure and confused on the other, namely: something that is not an idea at all – intuitions. We have seen that an intuition may be quite clear in its detection of ambiguity, i.e. its detection of the *existence* of two (or more) different meanings of a sign, without fully knowing what those meanings are. While such an intuition may be obscure as to conceptual content, therefore it is not at all confused; it does not confuse these contents, rather it rescues us from the potential confusion produced by a contradiction. To recap: the contradiction in each case results from interpreting it linguistically, i.e. imposing the logical principle of identity upon repetitions of the same sign, whereas release from this confusion requires the discernment of ambiguity amongst those repetitions. It is intuition that fosters this, and I shall contend that such a faculty of intuition provides a good candidate for the medieval 'cloud of unknowing', for Eckhart's obscure knowledge of the soul and, finally, for the comprehension of Brahman described in the Kena Upanishad.

Moreover, this employment of intuition may not be confined only to interpreting paradoxical words and phrases, but may assist us in the practical decisions of life. On the modern rational view it might at first appear that the contradictory or enigmatic nature of wise utterances must render them incapable of practical application. For it is hard, on the face of it, to see what has latterly been hinted, namely that a contradiction might lead to prudence or discretion in our actions. Is wisdom then only a matter of playing with words, having no practical value and bestowing no particular benefits? On the contrary, we shall see that what may have appeared merely as whimsical paradox may now be perceived to possess the deepest practical significance.

Whenever two people have a dispute this means that for some thought *p* asserted by one person, the other person must be asserting *not-p*, otherwise there is no dispute. What is bivocally a dispute or conflict might, therefore, be experienced by a single neutral observer as a contradiction. Now how can intuition help resolve such a dispute? Perhaps by detecting that what one person asserts or demands is not necessarily the contrary of what the other person asserts, even though they use the same words. This is the detection of ambiguity, much as was required for us to understand the paradoxical utterances above.

Recognizing ambiguity can mean seeing how not only the same word but also the same action or event can be treated as a sign interpretable in different ways. This recognition can be especially important when the same words or deeds, if performed by different people, may give rise to possible misunderstandings. Such even-handedness is clearly relevant to questions of *justice*, which require us to make fair and balanced judgements over conflicting views of the same situation. This can be amply illustrated by the legendary wisdom of Solomon, king of Israel around 950 BC. In one celebrated example, described in the Bible, two women both claimed the same baby as their own and Solomon offered to cut the baby in two and give them both half. Upon hearing this, one woman yielded the child to the other woman, thus revealing to Solomon that she was the real mother because she did not want the baby harmed.

I shall suggest that the wisdom of a judge in such situations is often the ability to detect ambiguity, i.e. the faculty of intuition capable of splitting one apparent concept disputed by two parties into two or more contrary concepts. Let us assume, in this case, that the two women manifested similar outward signs of love for the baby, so that these signs would be interpreted, initially, in the same way. Then initially in Solomon's mind the two claims that each woman is the mother would create a contradiction. Solomon knew there must be a difference between a mother's love and the love of any other woman – but what? Call these kinds of love, as we have previously done with paradoxes, *love-1, love-2* respectively. He was now aware of an ambiguity in the outward signs of love. Next, the story fuses the mental deliberation with physical drama: the aha moment in which the intuition of ambiguity gives way to splitting the initial concept of love into two clear contraries is surely being symbolized by the threat to cut the child in two. For the dichotomy discerned by Solomon was that while many women may desire to bond with a child, only the mother cares for something even more than this – the welfare of the child. The other woman's love may have been conditional on her being loved in return, but the mother's love is not conditional on this. Thus we may conclude that:

love-1 = caring for a child's well-being, and *love-2* = bonding with a child.

If both women expressed the same signs of love for the baby then, if there were only one kind of love, both women by these criteria would love the baby equally, contrary to maternal love being greater. Solomon, however, saw how to split these inconsistent criteria of love into two new concepts and hence eliminate the contradiction. Resolving the ambiguity, this states that one woman wants the well-being of the baby, but the other woman only wants to bond with a baby; in these two statements there is no longer any contradiction.

To summarize this example of practical wisdom, two new concepts of love have been created from an old concept merely by applying *intuition* to a practical conflict. By demonstrating a difference between the feelings of the two women, Solomon's wisdom was such that he was thereby able to see an inconsistency in the very criteria of love itself, providing an ambiguity by means of which to eliminate the contradiction. As in the various paradoxes, it was his detection of an ambiguity *that constituted his wisdom,* enabling him to split the current confused concept down the middle, to eliminate the apparent contradiction. This sundering of concepts was vividly symbolized in the Bible by the physical threat to split the baby itself down the middle. While the end result was a shrewd and prudent judgement, notice that no amount of prudent logical reasoning from the existing confused concept of love would have been adequate to produce it, since conceptual innovation was what was required.

Chapter 7

Shakespeare, Plato

Like the paradoxical sentences we have been examining, it may be said that more substantial constructs, viz works of art and literature, also have a hidden meaning or message, additional or contrary to the meanings of their parts. Indeed, we may say that what makes a mere picture into a work of art is the existence of an additional meaning, so that the obvious or representational meaning functions *symbolically* or as a metaphor for an additional higher or deeper meaning. Similarly literature or poetry are to be distinguished from mere stories or verse by the fact that, while composed only of words, their strictly verbal meanings can nevertheless, in combination, symbolize a deeper non-verbal meaning. As with the paradoxes we have lately considered, we may therefore say that works of literature too convey, by means of words, meanings that cannot be put into words. I put the matter thus because if the meaning of the artwork could be fully explained then we would have no need of the artwork. More accurately, we may say that our need for works of art would be less clearly distinguished from our need for ordinary representations. As with jokes and paradoxes, it is clear that we can often nevertheless describe how the mind reacts to parts of the artwork; this is the function of the art critic. But of course, we cannot simply replace the artwork by the criticism; the mind still itself needs to react in the anticipated fashion if the artwork is to be understood.

A Shakespearean sonnet

Works of art therefore possess, like jokes and paradoxes, non-verbal meaning. Typically, however, this meaning is only grasped gradually by contemplation: when reading the novel, listening to the music or gazing at a painting. Unlike jokes or one-line paradoxes, there is not likely to be an aha moment in which this meaning is grasped in a flash; often the process of realization in these more substantial cases resembles more a process of meditation. If there is an aha, we might say it is slowed down and is no longer transient and for this reason may seem more profound. However, it surely remains a mode of understanding other than thought; so the question arises: in these more substantial cases, is the hidden meaning of a work of art still tantamount to understanding a contradiction? Often, for instance, a novel may seem to be balancing several alternative or even conflicting views of the same situation. As a concrete example in which this does seem to be the case, we consider a particularly didactic kind of poem, the sonnet. A sonnet is a fourteen-line poem that is explicitly intended to explore a pair of contrasting ideas or themes, which might even come into conflict. We are going to examine in detail one sonnet in particular, Shakespeare's sonnet 94:

> They that have the pow'r to hurt and will do none,
> That do not do the thing they most do show,
> Who, moving others, are themselves as stone,
> 4 Unmoved, cold, and to temptation slow;
> They rightly do inherit heaven's graces
> And husband nature's riches from expense;
> They are the lords and masters of their faces,
> 8 Others but stewards of their excellence.
> The summer's flow'r is to the summer sweet,
> Though to itself it only live and die;
> But if that flow'r with base infection meet,
> 12 The basest weed outbraves his dignity:
> For sweetest things turn sourest by their deeds;
> Lilies that fester smell far worse than weeds.

The sonnet partly achieves its meaning by the use of a precise structure. If each line in the sonnet is denoted by a single letter, then the above poem has the rhyming sequence:

abab

cdcd

efef

gg

Here the lines are presented in groups of four (*quatrains*) and so the fourteen lines comprise three quatrains and a final couplet, and this structure is crucial to its overall meaning. The poem is regarded as notoriously obscure and, at the same time, one of Shakespeare's more important sonnets; for this reason its interpretation is regarded as particularly challenging. Many of Shakespeare's sonnets were inspired by his relationships with a youth and with a 'dark lady', towards whom the poems are undoubtedly directed; consequently they are tinged, in the light of these relationships, with various emotions, such as irony or reproach. However, I should say at the outset that in this sonnet at least I believe Shakespeare is using the stimulus of these feelings in order to address universal themes, and it is only these themes that I shall examine in providing the meaning of the poem. My analysis will be, therefore, entirely impersonal, having no reference whatever to the poet's personal relationships. Rather, I plan to relieve the enigmatic quality of the poem by employing those considerations lately introduced in the clarification of paradoxes. I believe that at the end of this analysis the meaning of the poem will thereby become transparently obvious. For, not only will we identify the dialectical content traditional to a sonnet, we will identify an explicit contradiction, which Shakespeare appears to resolve by working towards entirely new concepts. It is because of the novelty necessary for this interpretation, I believe, that the poem has seemed so problematic.

In the traditional sonnet a particular idea or theme is initiated in the opening lines. There is then normally a later point in the poem at which a new and contrasting idea is introduced; this is called the *volta* or 'turn' in the direction of the poem. The overall theme of sonnet 94 is the relative virtues and vices of self-restraint in human affairs, and the volta takes place at line 9, after the second quatrain. Here, the attitude of the poet shifts significantly, and so I shall refer to the remaining six lines as part II, with the first two quatrains being referred to as part I of the poem.

It is possible to grasp parts I, II separately, and so not perceive the volta, by seeing the floral imagery of part II as a metaphor for human action independent of the considerations in part I. The sonnet would then appear as two separate poems; however, if we do compare the lord with the lily, the steward with the weed etc., then we find in part II not only a metaphorical statement about human action, but one that contradicts the statement made in part I.

Let us now consider the sonnet in some detail. The poem begins by extolling the virtues of self-restraint in the case of those who have the power to hurt others (line 1) but refrain from doing so. In the first quatrain the poet elaborates on what this means: such a lord does not react in the obvious way to circumstances (line 2). Indeed, they may not *show* any feelings at all (line 3) and so find it easy (line 4) to resist *temptation*.

The second quatrain explains why this kind of behaviour is a good thing. The poet argues that it is good both morally and materially (lines 5, 6). Firstly, it is the kind of self-control needed to obey religious edicts and perform moral duties (such as resisting temptation), and hence will earn *heaven's graces* (line 5). Secondly, the poet hints that this requisite self-restraint typifies those of noble birth, for he says they *rightly do inherit* heaven's graces. But not only is this restrained conduct held to be morally excellent, it is also materially beneficial (line 6) since only by self-discipline will our plans succeed, bringing us *nature's riches from expense.*

Finally, part I ends what has appeared to be a somewhat feudal and religious view of the world lingering from the middle ages, by affirming that the key to a person being morally and physically superior is perfect self-restraint, characterized by the ability (line 7) to hide one's feelings. People (line 8) who do not possess this primary virtue merely minister to the excellence of those who do.

However, I shall argue that in part II Shakespeare takes a distinctly more modern approach. Admittedly the volta given by the opening couplet:

The summer's flow'r is to the summer sweet,
Though to itself it only live and die;

does little to hint at a shift of attitude. Martin[1] remarks that these lines 'look deceptively simple, and I am probably not the only reader to have carried them away singing in his head but have had no idea of their function in the poem as a whole.' They are indeed the calm before the storm, and the change in wind direction is surely this: that not only does the sweetness of the whole summer depend for its existence on the sweetness of each individual flower, but also the sweetness of any given flower depends for its existence upon *the contribution it makes to the summer* as a whole. In this way, the above couplet is indeed pivotal, a turning point for the whole poem, for it says that the value of a lily (lord) or a weed (steward) is no longer to be judged purely by their personal attainments, or how they were born, but on what they do for others. This is a distinctly modern or democratic view, in contrast with the feudal view lately explicated.

We are now ready to consider the finale of the poem. In the floral image, a flower such as a lily is beautiful if it represents a (possibly high-born) person possessing self-restraint, and a flower is plain like a weed if it represents a lowly undisciplined person. It is the smell of the flower not its looks, however, that represents the real quality of the person. And just as the sweet scent of a flower does not depend only on its appearance, so in part II it seems the real value of a person does not depend only on the self-restraint he exhibits, as the poet appears initially to have believed in part I of the sonnet. For if a disciplined lord becomes morally corrupted (meets base infection, line 11), so that perhaps he does now hurt others (contrary to the situation in line 1), then even the most lowly undisciplined person (weed) is a better man than he is (lines 12, 13). Thus, part II of the poem appears to contradict part I.

This certainly seems to be what the poem is saying, but Shakespeare gives no reason why a corrupt nobleman should be so much worse than an erring steward (undisciplined weed), other than perhaps the simple disillusionment, or even shock, at one so self-restrained, contrary to all expectation, lapsing in this way. However, I shall argue that the poem does convey a more substantial reason why this should be so, experienced sublimi- nally by *intuition*, that is never mentioned by Shakespeare explicitly. For, even if my own analytic interpretation be accepted as correct, what I should like to add is that, however exhaustive such an analysis may seem, it cannot in any case give us the full meaning of the poem, for then we would not need the poem itself, which clearly we do.

As I have hinted, something about the erring lord is evidently not being expressed by the above prose explanation. In other words, each reader or hearer has to understand the poem for herself, with or without the benefit of an explanation. The process of understanding will then be something more prolonged and contemplative than a brief aha moment. In fact I shall try to argue something unexpected: that with the meaning of this particular poem Shakespeare achieves the cognitive feat of conveying to the reader the possibility of a new concept that may previously have been unfamiliar. Thus, instead of the sonnet wholly being grasped via concepts, we grasp non-conceptually the possibility of a *future concept* which we do not yet possess. In this way poetry may sometimes be said to anticipate prose, for of course prose can only express thoughts if it possesses the concepts to do so.

Firstly, let us notice that if we do grasp the poem as a whole, then this grasp must be non-conceptual, as the two halves of the poem contradict each other and so cannot be combined in a thought. This is basically because part I seems to say self-restraint is *always* admirable, whereas part II says that, in the case of the festering lily, it is a bad thing. It may seem that the lord in part I is immune to this criticism, since we have interpreted the *festering lily* to mean someone who hurts others, and so this cannot really refer to a person with *the pow'r to hurt and will do none*. Hence the two parts of the sonnet might appear to be independent.

However, a milder interpretation of the festering lily is possible, in which others need not be hurt, thereby making it relevant to part I, as follows. The volta (lines 9–10) says florally that the lord is only excellent (sweet) if he communicates with the world and shares his gifts. The sin of ignoring others therefore would not be any serious moral corruption hurting them, but simply the sin of being aloof and self-centred; it is a sin of omission, the sin of pride. And of course, self-control would enable him to shut himself off from the world (and from the poet) all the more effectively. Thus we see, in this case, that the *base infection* festering and leaving a bad smell might be nothing more than pride and self-centredness. But, if so, then it does nevertheless come into conflict with the manifest excellence claimed for such a controlled (but non-hurting) lord in part I.

The resounding climax of the sonnet, the final couplet, which Martin[1] vividly described as a 'hammer-blow':

For sweetest things turn sourest by their deeds;
Lilies that fester smell far worse than weeds.

then concentrates the early misgivings of the volta into a contra-diction. For the poet initially seems to have believed that self-restraint was universally good, but now passionately disbelieves this, a contradiction. However, like the examples of one-line paradoxes, we may still feel that we do nevertheless *understand both parts of the poem at once*; and this understanding is, I shall claim, in fact the real meaning of the poem. Clearly the whole poem cannot be understood by thought, since no contradiction ever expresses a thought; and yet somehow this meaning must combine together the social responsibility of part II with the self-control of part I.

A first attempt at a resolution might, as with the paradoxes, be to split the concept of excellent or admirable behaviour into two kinds: personal excellence and social excellence. Then an arrogant lord might be said, without any contradiction, to excel in a personal sense, but not necessarily in a social sense. This realization is brought to us by the dialectic explored by the poem. But the impression given by the sonnet is surely that Shakespeare was seeking just *one key to all excellent behaviour*, not two different kinds of excellence.

Now such a concept, if there is one, cannot be logically definable solely in terms of self-restraint (part I), since this takes no account of the requirements of social responsibility (part II). And equally, the concept is not logically definable in terms of only the needs of society, since we cannot deduce, merely from these, anything about the value of individual self-restraint. Of course, we might believe that the intention of the poem is simply, via the festering lily, to deny universal merit to self-control by means of a *Reductio ad Absurdum* argument (see Chapter 6), and reject part I altogether. Surely, however, Shakespeare aimed rather to present a unifying view, somehow balancing the claims of parts I, II against each other. And yet, there is no way to *logically* combine parts I, II to define the desired concept, since these have already been shown to mutually contradict. If parts I,

II are to combine, this must be by selecting logical elements of part I to assemble with elements of part II into a new logical order, perhaps via an intuition invoked by the poem as a whole, but not mentioned by it.

One such compromise intuition arising from the poem by combining its elements differently might be that self-control is neither all good nor all bad, but is a mixed blessing: it is good if the action being controlled is good, and bad (overlooked in part I) if the action being controlled is bad. But we can go further than this, and discern a suggestion in the poem as to why self-restraint should have this effect. By dismantling human action into its constituent parts of means/ends, good/bad motives etc., alluded to in the poem, we might conceive an implied link between self-control, and the efficiency of a means to its end. For example, we may conceive that a disciplined lord might always be more efficient than an undisciplined person *at whatever end he pursues.* The poem might induce this intuition by its statement that the lord conserves 'nature's riches from expense' (line 6), carrying perhaps the suggestion that he can use these riches for any purpose he pleases, good or ill. Hence, if the lord wishes for instance to hurt people, as in part II, it surely follows that he would be able to do so the more effectively by employing self-discipline *to ill effect* than can the undisciplined steward. If I am right about this non-logical intuition being conveyed by the sonnet, then self-restraint, which in part I was so admired by the poet as an end in itself, might now be seen more as an instrument to be used either for good or for ill. None of this though is mentioned explicitly in the sonnet, but seems to be communi-cated non-logically, as our own response, arising naturally from the contradiction.

If these hints at the possibility of a new concept of human behaviour were to be finally crystallized, it does appear that Shakespeare is conveying by means of a self-contradiction some such intuition as that the best people can also become the worst when morally corrupted; because what is common to both the best and worst of people is the efficacy with which their intentions are carried out, for good or for bad respectively. And this efficacy is provided by self-discipline, which would now be seen potentially as much characteristic of a very bad person as of a very good person. For while the very best (sweetest) deeds (line 13) are efficiently good, so the very worst (sourest) deeds would equally be efficiently bad. In this case, subliminally, self-control would thus be seen as a kind of *amplifier* for human action, magnifying its good effects when good, and its bad effects when bad.

I am not suggesting that the poem in any sense makes this statement, only that it hints at this possibility amongst others. It is the detection merely of such new possibilities as these that constitutes our understanding of the poem, releasing us from the contradiction between part I and part II. The explicit interpretation just articulated would probably be a concept new to Shakespeare's readers and perhaps even to Shakespeare himself, since he seems unaware of it in part I of the sonnet, and in any case, never describes the concept explicitly, but only communicates it, if at all, by the poem as a whole. This whole presents a contradiction, and it seems to be the exact mechanism of this contradiction, the artistry that went into its construction, that is responsible for the hidden meaning of the poem. For clearly, not all contradictions have hidden meaning; most are just nonsense because they lack the appropriate artistry in their creation.

Dialectical reasoning

Thus it seems that a poem can evoke in the reader some comprehension of new concepts that cannot be defined logically in terms of any of the readers' existing concepts. Grasping the poem by intuition as an organic whole gives readers some insight into a *future understanding* of concepts they do not yet possess. A guarantee that the concept would indeed be new is that the intuition stems from a dialectical contradiction within the poem, for this ensures that it cannot be defined logically from statements made within the poem itself. The mechanism of the particular contradiction then seems to intimate to us how the poem can be broken down into simpler concepts which can then be recombined in new ways.

This ability of poetry to communicate beyond the limits of logic seems to suggest there can be a mystical element to the formation of rational concepts. For the above hypothetical concept of self-control as a mixed blessing was perfectly rational, and yet it was communicated only by the intuition arising from a contradiction between previously familiar concepts, as if it were a gift from heaven. The sonnet might thus perhaps be said to express a Socratic dialectic between its two parts, akin to that between theory and observations. Dialectic was a philosophical method of question and answer developed by Plato (350 BC), the main founder of Western philosophy. Using his own teacher Socrates as his central character, he wrote dialogues exploring the real meaning of concepts such as courage, knowledge or friendship. Now, in the light of this, perhaps we can regard Shakespeare's sonnet as an exercise in dialectic. For, if we imagine the poet of part I and the poet of part II to be two different voices, then maybe the whole sonnet can be viewed as part of a Socratic dialogue between two theories of human action.

Adopting Hegelian terminology, part I of the sonnet might be said to express the thesis, and part II its antithesis, contradicting it. The interesting result of the contradiction, obtained by combining shared elements of the two theses in new ways, might then be termed the synthesis. The dialectical method, if pursued sincerely, led said Plato to 'absolute truth'. Yet dialectic, for Plato, was something more than just logical reasoning, for it is ultimately not describable:

It is not something that can be put into words like other branches of learning; only after long partnership in a common life devoted to this very thing does truth flash upon the soul, like a leaping spark, and once it is born there it nourishes itself thereafter.

Plato, *The Seventh Letter*

Like Buddhist enlightenment, the mind must be in a suitably receptive state before the true nature of dialectic can be grasped. In any dialogue, Plato seems to be saying, it is only the rapport between the participants that allows the dialectical argument to produce real understanding. But what, apart from the conclusion of the logical reasoning, is there to understand? Perhaps the apparent contradictions between the various theses and antitheses advanced by the speakers, en route to that conclusion. It seems Plato believed that despite, or because of, this friction, the participants can generate the 'leaping spark' of a common understanding, because they are all sincere seekers after truth. As with Shakespeare's sonnet, it appears that more was communicated by a Socratic dialogue than was actually said by it.

If this analogy between the sonnet and the bivocal essence of Plato's dialogues is upheld, then a consequence would be that Socratic dialogues may not, after all, be wholly deductive as is normally assumed. This is because the conclusion or synthesis is not always contained entirely in the theses and antitheses (the premises assumed by the speakers and questioner in the dialogue). Rather, it may be, as we have seen, a mutual creative leap in the minds of the speakers coaxed by intuition from the contradictions into which Socrates leads them all. Hence Socrates cannot always be regarded merely as defining or clarifying pre-existing concepts (such as courage) shared by all the participants in the dialogue from the outset, but *may himself have been engaged in conceptual change*, significantly altering the very concept under discussion, and employing dialogue as an instrument of such change. The conclusion would then be about this new concept rather than the original ones, while possibly still bearing the same name. This may more accurately have been what Plato meant by his belief that dialectic reveals the true nature of concepts, for it shows one way in which new concepts may be created. And whereas, for Plato, the ultimate clarity provided by the pure light of reason was only given by dialogue, and includes a grasp of how contradictions can lead to new concepts, we have also seen that, for Descartes, the light of reason was provided only by monologues using existing concepts, in which contradictions were to be avoided at all costs.

Notice here that dialogue need not only be social, but can be entirely internal to one person, exploring two viewpoints via a bivocal thought process. To then see the difference between the expressive powers of monologue and private dialogue, consider that each of the paradoxes we have recently been examining, whilst literally meaningless as thoughts in a Cartesian monologue, may nevertheless give rise to a Socratic dialogue. For example, *Everybody's friend is nobody's friend* can be understood via the Platonic conception of the mind, embracing dialogue, but not by the Cartesian conception. We demonstrate the former by noticing that the bivocal resolution to the paradox can be expressed not only privately, but also as a *social dialogue*, which begins with one speaker (voice) believing it is possible for x to be everybody's friend, whilst another speaker believes this to be impossible. Of course, as with the doctor and the patient, the onlooker or reader has the dilemma of attempting to grasp both interpretations of 'friend' at the same time. Nevertheless, it is a debate that can surely be played out in a single mind, by privately employing two different 'voices'.

The dialogue (public or private) in this case might proceed by speaker 1 claiming the possibility of being universally popular, and speaker 2 objecting by arguing that by trying to help a pair of rivals, one must inevitably offend one and probably both of them. Speaker 1 then might reply that, as long as one doesn't try to help, one can like and be liked by both of them and, indeed, everybody. This should lead truth to 'flash upon the soul' of both speakers, as they make the sudden or gradual discovery that friendship entails more than mere goodwill, and that indeed there are two kinds of friendship: casual friendship, based only upon liking each other, and close friendship, based also upon helping each other. Furthermore, that what speaker 1 meant had all along contradicted what speaker 2 had meant; thus the discussion had more resembled peace negotiations over contested territory, rather than the elucidation of mutually shared ideas. If indeed Socrates were the benign diplomat leading the discussion he might then also observe that by trying to be a close friend of everybody, one would end up a close friend of nobody, since everybody is in competition with somebody, and one can't help one without opposing the other. Finally, both speakers might then be brought to agree that everybody's casual friend would necessarily be nobody's close friend, since a casual friend is never a close friend. As a matter of fact, Socrates does lead one of Plato's dialogues on the subject of friendship (the *Lysis*), but along completely different lines.

A dialogue of this type may be said to spell out in a public and incremental form the private logical processes previously conjectured to occur when grasping a paradox in a flash, during an aha moment. This demonstrates that two 'voices' are necessary in order to express the meanings of the paradoxes, and that their content cannot adequately be expressed by a straight-forward prose narrative, or monologue. Whether conveyed by paradox or by dialogue, the end result might be a genuine insight for all the speakers, in the sense that such insight into the mechanisms of friendship might have been hitherto unknown. In which case our hypothetical Socrates might be said to have effected a minor local conceptual change.

With respect to major conceptual change, Socratic dialogue may also have unexpected relevance to modern scientific thinking, for it may present an analogy with the empirical progress of science. In the previous case of the sonnet, we may notice that the concepts of self-restraint, social responsibility, were *incommensurable* with each other, and that the conceptual change expressed in the poem resembles one of the scientific revolutions described by TS Kuhn. One such example from the history of science concerns the physical nature of *fire*. Noting that things are visibly consumed by flames leaving only charred remains, one theory naturally assumed that something (termed *phlogiston*) was removed from objects during the blaze. However, we may say this theory was *contradicted* by certain observations, such as the fact that the weight of things sometimes increased when they were burnt. This produced an additional complication to the theory since it seemed to require the view that phlogiston could sometimes have negative weight. Such observational contradictions are referred to by Kuhn as *anomalies* in the theory.

The problem was solved in the eighteenth century by the French chemist Lavoisier, who proved, on the contrary, that something, oxygen, is actually *added* to objects when they burn. Thus, when wood is burnt, the oxygen in the air combines with the hydrogen and some of the carbon in the wood to produce CO_2 and H_2O, leaving behind most of the carbon as charred remains. We can see that Lavoisier's discovery has the character of *conceptual change*, in which the concept of phlogiston was displaced by the concept of oxygen, where neither was definable in terms of the other.

So perhaps, like sonnet 94, in which a new concept arose from a contradiction, it is possible to see that, inside the mind, only under the influence of a contradiction (anomalous observations), not by any logical thought process, could Lavoisier's intuition of oxygen have been generated from the phlogiston theory. For it did not follow logically from any theory which preceded it, and indeed it contradicted the phlogiston theory. In this way, we can perhaps view conceptual change in science also as a dialectical argument: between conflicting theories for the same observations. And here, as in poetry, contradictions need not be meaningless, but may gain their meaning from the part they play in anticipating particular future concepts.

My plan, however, is to show how such intuitions of conceptual change are not confined either to poetry or to science, but are a routine part of everyday life. The implication is that conceptual change is not really as exceptional as we take it to be, but happens in minor ways, all the time.

Chapter 8

Conflict Situations

In daily life the disinterested pursuit of truth for its own sake is a rarity, rather than the norm. Debate is less likely to be of a scientific or Socratic nature, than verbal arguments harnessed to the pursuit of private interests. Consequent disagreements need not in these cases lead to any mutually satisfactory outcome. But in all disputes there is nevertheless one thing that is normally agreed upon, and that is the meanings of the terms used. Indeed that is surely a prerequisite for any dispute: there must first be a shared repertoire of concepts by which to frame any disputed proposition or thought, p. Then one disputant believes or desires to bring about p, and the other believes or desires *not-p*. Although there may be several disputants, they often share a common language of argument, with little or no evident interest or willingness to alter this language.

However, what we have seen in the case of academic discussions is how, when examining contradictory assertions, the wisdom of a Socrates can sometimes make agreement possible by altering the meanings of one or more of the words in the contradiction. I shall now show how this can also be applied to practical conflicts: if we can show that two disputants do not, after all, mean quite the same thing, then we have a basis for resolving their conflict.

Military conflict

Consider, for example, a war between two countries Aphla, Ateb. Suppose that Ateb attacks Aphla from commanding heights x overlooking Aphla, but Aphla successfully repels the Ateb invasion and in the process seizes the high ground x. In peace negotiations Aphla argues that x now belongs to Aphla, but Ateb argues that x still rightfully belongs to Ateb. How can a diplomat resolve this dispute? The diplomat must somehow reconcile the beliefs both that x belongs to Aphla, and that x belongs to Ateb, a contradiction. However, when the diplomat proceeds to engage in negotiation with both parties, he discovers that the reason Aphla feels entitled to x is not merely as the spoils of war, but because they believe that, if occupied by Ateb, the commanding heights of x pose a permanent threat to Aphla and so Aphla feels a need to occupy x for its own protection. On the other hand of course, Ateb feels entitled to x because historically and culturally x always has been part of Ateb. For the sake of this discussion we may suppose that x is uninhabited scrubland of little or no agricultural use, so that the main reason Ateb desires x is out of national sovereignty, and perhaps mineral rights.

Now there is no way of combining the two demands for x in a logical fashion so as to satisfy both parties. However, let us now imagine the diplomat has an aha moment in which, although Aphla, Ateb say they want the same thing, he perceives nevertheless that what Aphla wants differs from what Ateb wants. For Aphla wants what might be termed a 'buffer zone' protecting it from attack or invasion by Ateb, while Ateb wants national sovereignty and economic ownership of x; and moreover, he perceives that it may yet be possible to reconcile these two aims where it was not at all possible to reconcile them both having total control over x. For it may be possible, in return for Aphla acknowledging the legitimate sovereignty of Ateb over x and ownership of its economic resources, for Ateb to agree to allow the UN or even Aphla itself to patrol x, ensuring x remains essentially demilitarized. Ateb need not agree to this in perpetuity, but perhaps only for a limited period, renewable on mutually agreeable terms. Thus, instead of an intractable conflict, the negotiations now become the relatively milder and more tractable debate about terms of renewal.

In this way the diplomat has split the concept of sovereignty into a military concept and an economic concept, so that x may be said to 'belong' to Aphla in the first sense but not in the second sense. The unilateral concept of sovereignty which was once so potent has now been eroded and lost some of its powers; the diplomat has effected conceptual change, a change furthermore which could be lifesaving. And, although this is a very different context, notice that he achieved this result, not by logical reasoning alone, but by the same aha faculty as used in the appreciation of jokes, poems and paradoxes. The diplomat has put Socratic dialogue, as I have construed it in terms of conceptual change, to practical effect.

If acceptable to both parties, this may assuredly be seen by them as an example of wise judgement by the diplomat. Wisdom may thus be distinguished from knowledge by noting that knowledge consists of true thoughts employing current mutually agreed concepts, whereas wisdom seems to seek out new concepts by accepting contradictions between current concepts. No contradiction can ever provide an example of knowledge, since it never expresses a single thought; but it is nevertheless the keystone of wisdom. Hence wisdom is a kind of understanding not expressible in thought. It is beyond concepts, for the very reason that it is engaged in creating concepts.

National treasures

We now consider a non-military example of the same thing. Suppose over a hundred years ago a colonial power Patria purchased artefacts deriving from the site of an ancient civilization in one of its colonies. A dispute arises after decolonization between the modern country Kustan occupying the same site, and the ex-colonial power Patria, as to the rightful ownership of the artefacts. Kustan says the artefacts are part of their national and cultural heritage and should never have been sold. Patria says they belong to the whole world, and in any case were purchased lawfully by agreement with the original landowner at the time. Moreover Kustan, being a young country, is not politically stable, whereas Patria is a mature democracy and so is a safe and secure custodian of the artefacts on behalf of the world.

So we see there is a dispute between various kinds of claims to the artefacts; how could they all be acknowledged by a suitable arbiter? It might for example be conceded by Kustan that Patria is the economic owner and a secure custodian, but Kustan might feel particularly strongly that they should be returned physically to their native soil on Kustan, as their proper place of origin, and not be uprooted thousands of miles into an alien environment. So one novel proposal by an arbiter, to accommodate these differing claims, might be perhaps that a remote branch of the national museum of Patria be opened in Kustan, thus exhibiting the artefacts in Kustan permanently. In this way, the artefacts would be returned to their natural home in Kustan, while still being owned and protected by Patria. Or perhaps the exhibition might be viewed as only temporary, transitional to a full transfer of ownership, perhaps dependent on the proven political stability of Kustan. Of course, any forcible seizure of this outpost of the Patria museum by Kustan would constitute an international incident. Perhaps the museum might be administered as part of the Patrian embassy in Kustan. Eventually, Patria might agree to cede ownership of the artefacts to Kustan, perhaps on payment of compensation, and privileged access to these, and other similar artefacts, in the future.

As with the military example, the concept of ownership as exclusive control has been eroded to enable privileges of different kinds for interested parties. In this way, an apparent logical contradiction has, in both cases, been eroded by conceptual change.

The Cuban Missile Crisis
For a real-life example of how wisdom literally saved the world,

we need look no further than how President Kennedy handled the Cuban Missile Crisis. In 1962 US spy planes revealed the existence of Soviet ballistic missiles in Cuba, posing a nuclear threat to the continental USA on its own doorstep, not allowing time for their interception. Since there were already American nuclear missiles in Italy and Turkey, the Soviet premier Khrushchev may have seen Cuba as redressing the imbalance. But whether this was indeed the case, or whether it was the Cuban missiles that upset the balance of power as most of Kennedy's advisers believed, the fact is that Kennedy had to do something, for in the fraught mood of the moment not to have acted at all might have invited impeachment, or even the possibility of a military coup. His joint chiefs of staff were all calling for air strikes against the launch pads, or a full-scale invasion of Cuba. Doing nothing was therefore not an option.

And yet Kennedy was acutely aware that attacking Soviet troops directly could put the whole world in peril, for attack and counterattack could escalate uncontrollably into nuclear war. Hitherto, the Cold War had only been fought by proxy, in various other parts of the world, avoiding direct conflict. Now the two antagonists were in direct confrontation. But, at the same time, saner voices were counselling caution: at the other extreme Adlai Stevenson, the US representative to the UN, proposed to resolve the issue by quiet diplomacy, by exchanging personal envoys to negotiate a resolution. However, an immediate solution was required, and it was clear that no concrete concession could ever be guaranteed from such an ongoing dialogue. Accordingly, Stevenson was viewed by the military chiefs as an appeaser.

What emerged after 13 days of debate, however, was a wiser strategy: a middle way between the two extremes, first proposed, apparently, by Robert McNamara. This was the notion of a naval blockade of Cuba, designed to prevent further supplies of military hardware from reaching Cuba on Soviet ships. As the blockade came into effect, the world held its collective breath to see whether the Soviet and American navies would clash, possibly precipitating a war. In the event, most Soviet ships did not breach the American blockade but suddenly reversed their direction without a shot being fired, and the world breathed again.

The blockade had evidently been a brilliantly creative idea, which seems to have succeeded because it steered a middle course between military aggression on the one hand, and passive diplomacy on the other. It did this because:

- It was a military action, and yet was non-aggressive. It was an act of defence, not offence. By providing an imaginary barrier it invited the other side to commit an aggressive act by crossing it. Instead of invading enemy territory, the barrier created, so to speak, an artificial maritime 'territory', and then challenged the enemy to invade it. In this way, the roles of offence and defence were reversed.
- It was also a diplomatic action, in the sense that its implementation, via boarding parties, would have enabled face-to-face dialogue between the personnel of both navies.
- It was in international waters, and so was not in any sense an intrusion into Soviet supported territory, but was a wholly manufactured territory.
- The blockade was combined with a secret offer to withdraw all the American missiles from Turkey at a later date.

If air strikes or invasion had been the original military *thesis*, and quiet diplomacy its *antithesis* in a dialectic, then the naval blockade was surely a creative synthesis from their contradiction, not definable logically from either or both of these two extremes. Nevertheless, it combined elements of each in such a way as to avoid initiating violent conflict, thereby securing agreement between most of the advisers to the president. In this way, Kennedy's historic initiative conforms to our proposed definition of wisdom as a concept-modifying response to a logical contradiction.

Moral dilemmas

Reconciling the thoughts in a contradiction or clash of ideas can thus only be achieved by altering some of the concepts of which they are composed. I would suggest this may be true even of moral dilemmas. Consider, for example, the debate concerning those conditions, if any, under which abortion may be morally justified. Without pronouncing on this issue, let me just highlight a key factor in the debate.

Feminist groups tend to think of the human embryo, up to a certain stage, as a part of the mother's body over which she alone should have sovereign jurisdiction. The Catholic Church, on the other hand, thinks of the embryo as an independent human being having human rights, from the moment of conception onwards. These two points of view contradict each other as thesis and antithesis, and in any personal case it is an agonizing decision of life and death. However, to make a broad philosophical judgement on the possible circumstances for the legitimacy or otherwise of abortion in general, it is surely necessary to try to hold in mind at the same time these two conflicting interpretations of the embryo, despite the fact that they contradict each other.

While there can be no guarantee of an outcome, a Socratic dialogue might begin by analysing both opposing views into their conceptual elements, endeavouring to find common ground. It was in just this way that Shakespeare in sonnet 94 was able to view a man who hid his feelings both as exhibiting commendable self-restraint, and at the same time as failing to share his gifts with the world. In the abortion dilemma, we again have conflicting descriptions of the same situation, and our hope might be to find shared conceptual elements by which to formulate a 'middle way', i.e. an account of the situation that is completely new, but which draws upon the merits of both the existing accounts, while perhaps also disagreeing with both at crucial points.

One way forward might be to modify not one but both of the conflicting interpretations of the embryo by seeing it at certain stages as neither fully a human being, nor simply a part of a person's body. One might perhaps focus on the notion of independence, inquiring about the degrees of independence that might be exhibited by a part of someone's body. The purpose of this would be in order to reconceptualize the human embryo, if this were possible, using elements of both interpretations to produce a new concept, or synthesis, contrary to both. In this case the resulting concept would be a concept neither of a full human being, nor of a mere body part, but which might nevertheless be helpful in clarifying at what stage, and under what conditions, it may be morally justified to terminate a pregnancy.

Mental conflict

In each of the political and moral examples just considered, if no new concepts had been forthcoming we would just have had conflict. Thus Ateb might have been endlessly at war with Aphla over x, and Kustan might break off diplomatic relations with Patria, but the possible consequences over Cuba are simply unthinkable.

While conflict and its resolution may be experienced socially as war and peace, they can also be experienced within one person as mental conflict and peace of mind respectively. Indeed it is often conflicts or peace in the minds of powerful and influential leaders that result in social and political conflicts or peace respectively. Mental conflicts arise when we commit ourselves to inconsistent objectives. E.g. we may, in the name of equal opportunity, be opposed to private education, and yet we may want only the finest private education for our own child; this is a contradiction, resulting in a mental conflict or cognitive dissonance. Sartre says that to be an authentic individual, i.e. to live life honestly, such choices should always be faced squarely and made knowingly; this is why 'freedom is a burden'. And yet we know that spiritual freedom is light as a feather – how can this be?

In *Existentialism is a Humanism* (1946), Sartre provided the real-life example of a man living in occupied France, with his mother who depends upon him emotionally, but who now, however, has the chance of joining the Free French in England, which would entail deserting his mother. Sartre presents him as having the difficulty of choosing between supporting his mother, and supporting the liberation of his country. This is certainly a mental conflict, which as a free individual he cannot ignore. To not face the question, but merely drift into the most convenient option, is for Sartre not a choice 'made in the name of freedom' but is mere laziness. It is in this spirit of freedom that Sartre inquires, 'How do you think he could have decided, in perfect peace of mind, either to abandon his mother or remain with her? There is no means of judging.' However, I shall argue that, on the contrary, there is a means of judging.

Firstly I should like to ask: why does Sartre give the son only these two options, isn't this somewhat artificial? In reality there are many other possibilities for the son which might enable him to aid the French resistance without travelling too great a distance from his mother. Perhaps he could reduce risk to his mother by living in a different town, from which he might visit her periodically or even frequently, without the irrevocable separation of England. Or perhaps he could live with his mother but aid the resistance in passive ways, without arousing much suspicion. However, more interesting than this is why Sartre presents the choices in this artificial fashion, as a fait accompli. It is surely because this is how the options presented themselves to the son himself, that he saw his life in these categories, and that the son may not himself have been aware of the scope for modification. It is even possible that Sartre did not see this scope either, or for some reason discounted it. Could the reason be that it followed from Sartre's theory of the mind that, at any given time, the mind thinks of certain thoughts and not of others? And so Sartre is saying that, given that the son can only imagine these possibilities, he is forced to choose only amongst what he can imagine.

If the son was indeed unimaginative in his thoughts, then Sartre seems to be endorsing this lack of imagination by affirming that 'there is no means of judging' between the two options. It even seems as if any equivocation between these extremes by the son might be criticized by Sartre as vagueness or ambivalence. For, the kind of middle course being envisaged above will not be the result of clear thoughts in the mind of the son, since he may need to make it up as he goes along, reacting to events. Therefore these courses of action are, for Sartre, not freely chosen, since the required actions could not be performed in full knowledge of what he is doing, and so can only be actions he drifts into accidentally, or is pushed into. In Sartre's theory of freedom, authenticity requires us to faithfully choose between all the options we can honestly imagine; these options are determined by all the thoughts, p, we can clearly think.

But is there not a third possibility between clear decisions on the one hand, and ambivalence on the other, namely intuition? For if we can *understand* situations other than by thought, can we not also knowingly choose how to act by means other than thought? This is the proposal that I can freely and responsibly choose to act in a way not aimed at bringing about any clearly conceived state of affairs, p. In the above example, the 'Middle Way' compromise options are not clear thoughts in the son's mind, and Sartre seems to infer from this that no such options can be responsibly chosen by him. However, if we regard his two 'given' options as a thesis and antithesis, then, like the solutions to the other conflicts we have considered, such a course of action need not be vague or ambivalent, lazy or confused, but may be a conscientious 'Middle Way' which selects elements from the thesis and from the antithesis, but cannot be defined logically from either. Thus, it seems on Sartre's account that such a middle course, despite being perhaps the most rational and intelligent alternative, can nevertheless not be *freely* and responsibly chosen by the son as a possible course of action, simply because he is unable to formulate it clearly in thought. This is because, as I understand Sartre, only by enacting a clear thought, knowing fully that he is doing so, does a person act freely and responsibly. For one cannot be held responsible for what one cannot conceive, and one can only choose freely between the thoughts one is able to formulate.

However, surely Sartre must be wrong, for when we select a Middle Way it seems we certainly do know what we are doing, and may be acting fully responsibly and freely. Nonetheless, we are not acting as Sartre would wish, by executing either means or ends previously formulated in thought. Rather it feels as if our deeds are guided by a higher power in which we acquiesce, much like an artist selecting the individual brushstrokes for a painting. The artist may have no clear idea in mind of the finished painting, and so the brushstrokes are not selected as the rational means to any such goal; and yet each brushstroke is fully intended by the artist. What we can say is that the artist has an intuition about how to proceed and that, while he cannot predict which brushstroke to make, he certainly knows when he has done one right, since it contributes to the whole, whereas a wrong stroke jars with the whole.

We may say each brushstroke is a voluntary act, which is conceived neither as an end in itself, nor as a means to an end. Of course, it is indeed conceived as a means of producing some painting, but not as a means of producing this particular painting. Similarly in life, as in my suggestion for Sartre's example, no conceptual thought was possible for the son capable of formulating the middle course which resulted from his intuition, *otherwise it would then have been a third option for him,* which it wasn't. Rather, it might perhaps be considered the outcome of something that can only be described as a future concept for him, containing elements of each of the two current options, and which becomes gradually disclosed to him by his own actions.

If choosing a course of action in this manner can no longer qualify as existential freedom, perhaps we should, by our comparison with the artist, call it rather *spiritual freedom.* And, far from being a burden, this freedom is an exhilarating joy; exactly what you would expect from freedom. In other words, spiritual freedom corresponds more faithfully to the true meaning of freedom, as opposed to the travesty provided by existentialism, viewing freedom as hard work.

What is Man?

In the last example, the young man agonized over his choices, yet Sartre says there is no way of judging between them: because the two options contradict he must simply choose one of them, and accept responsibility; this is what Sartre has called the burden, the anguish, of freedom. In other words, the only internal significance of this contradiction is that it generates mental conflict. The reason for this, of course, traces back to the Cartesian belief that human understanding consists only of clear thoughts. This fatal assumption leads us to regard any mental activity in which clear thought is absent as confused or conflicted and hence unintelligible. Consequently, the existential void is an anguish entirely due to this Cartesian assumption that only clear and distinct ideas have any meaning; and since a contradiction never expresses a clear and distinct idea, no contradiction ever has any meaning. Liberation from the void of self-contradiction cannot be provided by any thought process, since this itself requires the very commitment to non-contradiction which generated fear of the void in the first place. Nevertheless, we have seen that by a different kind of understanding, by not making the Cartesian assumption, liberation from the contradictions and dilemmas of life may sometimes be possible.

Being alienated, i.e. being in conflict with 'the whole of life', really means believing that reality is wholly given by logically consistent facts, yet being also aware that one's own inmost being cannot be understood this way. Hence, believing that there appears to be a mismatch between oneself and the world, regardless of whatever the world happens to contain. For the Cartesian assumption entails that I cannot even know myself other than by thought, and Descartes himself famously drew exactly this conclusion in his *Cogito*. In the cartoon of Chapter 1, we now see that it may be the tramp's own commitment to factual information that prevents him knowing who he is or where he is going, perhaps by rejecting his own intuitions as self-contradictory. However, we have noted that as a result of these very contradictions we are sometimes able to alter these limits of factual thought – by altering the concepts to be employed in such thoughts. And surely, since it is I who alters the limits of my thoughts in this way, I cannot be merely identical either to the thoughts themselves (Hume), or to the thinker of those thoughts (Descartes). If anything, I may possibly be that which alters the limits to thought, i.e. that which forms new concepts by transgressing beyond those limits. For, it is only by its apparently contradictory nature that we know a concept to be new, since if that concept were expressible in terms of current concepts, then no contradiction would be encountered. The hallmark of the concept that is truly new is that whenever we try to express it in terms of our existing concepts, we inevitably contradict ourselves.

Now, the self-consciousness of thought can evidently be experienced only by means of those concepts we already possess.

It follows that during conceptual change we must be aware of ourself by means of *a different kind of self-awareness*; this is, for example, the awareness of self experienced during the aha moments of self-contradiction. These contradictory moments are moments, not of the void of incomprehension as the Cartesians would have us believe, but of comprehension of a new kind. But, if the meaningfulness of such paradoxes and poems as we have examined is rejected, then surely it is the heart and soul of us, our very humanity, that is being rejected. For it is in poetry, humour and paradox that we are at our most human; it is this fount and origin of all new meaning that seems to be the very nature of what we are, our innermost being.

And now it seems as if the essence of man is not the Cartesian *ens cogitans*, given only by his thoughts, for this is just his use of previously known concepts. Rather, it seems as if a fuller portrayal of man is as a creator of new concepts, a maker of those meanings from which such thoughts must be constructed. Perhaps this is the real meaning of 'sapiens' in *Homo Sapiens*, the real meaning of wisdom, as opposed to knowledge or thought. And, perhaps it is because the sense of self transcending knowledge and thought cannot be conceived by the self-conscious user, I, of current concepts, that the Buddhists refer to it as No-I. For, although I can possess such a *concept* of the transcendence of thought, nevertheless correctly ascribing this concept to myself is not sufficient to know myself as No-I; for knowing the latter also requires the mental act of actually transcending my thoughts. Similarly, even if the tramp in the cartoon were to be given this information about transcendence by the clerk, still this would not tell him who he is or where he is going; for that, as in grasping a joke, is something he needs to do for himself. To know oneself is thus revealed not so much by the use of one's current concepts as one's ability to recognize potential new meaning when our concepts conflict. To be unable to do this is surely the mark of ignorance or dissociation from oneself, for it is to only ever see in contradictions a lack of meaning, the void.

It does now seem that the delicate self-awareness experienced in grasping a paradox or a poem, or in wise judgement, answers better to entering 'most intimately into what I call *myself*' than what Hume himself attempted. Hume and his successors have been seeking the subject of perception and thought, while failing to separately distinguish from this the subject of humour, poetry and wisdom. This is a higher or spiritual sense of self clearly different from the thinker or subject of experience, the lower self; for it is a maker of concepts and not just a user of concepts. Of course, in drawing this distinction we are not distinguishing metaphysical entities, but simply referring to a higher sense of self-awareness, as opposed to the lower experience of self-consciousness. This sensitivity to poetry and paradox can surely lay claim to expressing my inmost being, namely: what I most intimately call myself.

Suffering

We can now perhaps see that it is not human 'freedom' as such but the denial of this intimate sense of self that creates the mental suffering which Sartre called 'anguish'. It is not our freedom in the use of concepts but, on the contrary, our imprisonment by those very concepts that brings anguish. Real spiritual freedom, however, as we might indeed expect, liberates; for it allows us to choose other options, beyond those confined by our current concepts. If, with the Cartesians, we censor as 'unintelligible' whatever mental choice does not express a clear thought, then we do not allow ourself even the chance of making that choice by intuition. These would include those apparently inconsistent choices which, instead of being nurtured as paradoxical, providing partial meanings in the present of fuller meaning in the future, we would condemn as being permanently meaningless and confused. Or else the inconsistency might provoke an ongoing anguish of mental conflict in the continuing present. Borrowing a term from Freud, we might call this bondage the *repression* of our higher self, repression of our spirituality. When such repression is total, the existential anguish of mental conflict can infect the whole of life, as expressed in this cry from Sylvia Plath:

> ... I am a conglomerate garbage heap of loose ends – selfish, scared, contemplating devoting the rest of my life to a cause – going naked to send clothes to the needy, escaping to a convent, into hypochondria, into religious mysticism, into the waves – anywhere, anywhere, where the burden, the terrifying hellish weight of self-responsibility and ultimate self-judgment is lifted.
> *The Journals of Sylvia Plath (1950–1962)*

The lure of a *cause*, for a person in such a state, is surely to ease the burden of decision-making, unknowingly inflicted by the act of repressing one's higher sense of self, of denying one's spirituality. For any such cause would automatically make the decisions of life for us, bringing blessed relief. It is indeed for such reasons that people, to relieve their inner turmoil, sometimes cling to fanaticism, or religious fundamentalism. Conforming to such a cause would according to Sartre be, therefore, an act of bad faith. Indeed, Plath's current life, facing the 'hellish weight of self-responsibility', would tragically be considered her only 'authentic' response. In the end it was all too much for her to bear, and she committed suicide at the age of thirty.

It is this kind of mental suffering that I believe the Buddha saw as the source of all the ills of the world, and wished to relieve. For it is plain, from cases such as this, that success or failure to attain enlightenment may well be a matter of life and death, and it seems vital for us to find some way to be less censorious with ourself. We surely need to let our poetic understanding or intuition, which is our very core and essence, have some influence therefore over our most ordinary practical decisions, i.e. the way we shape our life. What is variously called enlightenment, redemption or salvation would, for such a sufferer, surely be her unconditional acceptance of her own poetic intuition as having actual legitimate authority over her life, instead of rejecting it as not rationally acceptable, thereby repressing her inmost being. This acceptance always requires an act of self-surrender, surrendering the primacy of conceptual thought, surrendering the priority of logic and will over life, where these have predominated to a neurotic degree.

It is surely no coincidence that Sylvia Plath was a poet, and also it is surely because the aha experiences of intuition are so essential to humour, as well to the arts, that so many comedians, as well as writers and artists, have been prone to depression and suicide.

Chapter 9

Enlightenment

Eastern religions have for thousands of years prescribed an insight into ultimate meaning, and a consequent relief from the mental strife and anxieties of life, by the adoption of various spiritual practices, such as meditation, or chanting, or koans. What these practices have tended to have in common has been the desire to eliminate thought. Why? Because all thoughts, even religious thoughts, were viewed as superficial when compared to experience of the Tao itself, or the Atman, or later, to nirvana or the satori of Zen. This has mainly not been the case in the West, where the practices of Judaism, Christianity, Islam and philosophy since Plato have all sought to express themselves via thought (e.g. prayer), and any acknowledgement of mystical experience has never been allowed to disparage religious doctrine, but only enhance it.

Nevertheless, William James has similarly cited Christian visionaries such as John Bunyan, describing salvation as always requiring self-surrender, and abdicating from the devices of one's own thought and will. James describes a 'genuine saint' David Brainerd who says:

> One morning while I was walking in a solitary place as usual, I at once saw that all my contrivances and projects to effect or procure deliverance and salvation for myself were utterly vain; I was brought quite to a stand, as finding myself totally lost. I saw that it was forever impossible for me to do anything towards helping or delivering myself...
>
> ... then, as I was walking in a thick grove, unspeakable glory seemed to open to the apprehension of my soul.

However, as St Teresa had found, the perennial question for Christians always remains: for the resulting mystical leap of faith (the 'glory') what kind of comprehending is it (Chapter 3)?

At the heart of every major religion there does indeed seem to be a mystical tradition (e.g. Quietists in Christianity, Cabbalists in Judaism, Sufis in Islam). This is because, no matter how dogmatic a religion became, it was usually also one of its dogmas that there was something inexpressible that is even greater than the religion itself, since this was the reason for the existence of the religion. Buddhism, however, is noteworthy among the great religions of the world for the centrality of its mystical tradition. For, only in Buddhism is mysticism itself made the central object of thought and belief. By this I mean firstly that it is central to the religious mainstream, and not just confined to esoteric fringes of the religion. Secondly, that in Buddhism it is held not merely that the central object of belief is inexpressible (as with God, Allah), but that it is the very nature of inexpressibility itself which turns out to be the central object of belief.

Notwithstanding this difference, the route taken by many of the spiritual practices of both West and East has been to achieve holiness or mystical insight, in particular to change one's life, by completely altering one's state of mind; i.e. to *reject one's current way of thinking* and replace it by one not currently thinkable. And in each case, because of the noetic character of such mystical experience (Chapter 2), this salvation has always required the possibility of a form of understanding beyond thought. However, recognizing the need to eliminate thought, Indian logic for instance, has not sought to dispel contradictions as devoid of meaning, as the West has done. Indeed, as we found with Kena, it seemed that contradiction even became credible as a mode of self-expression; it was almost as if, in successfully preventing thought, the contradiction was itself the desired insight.

How was this believed to be possible? In Zen Buddhism contradiction became specifically acknowledged as possibly instrumental in the life-changing nature of enlightenment, by being explicitly incorporated into spiritual practices. It seems the reason for this development has been a recognition that only contradiction can eliminate the possibility of thought, and hence only contradiction can impose the necessity for a kind of understanding other than thought. This was part of the Buddha's vision from the start, for it was a vital part of his insistence that there is a state of mind, enlightenment, whose very nature is to be indescribable in words, and inconceivable in thought. Yet this enlightenment is nevertheless to be understandable and, indeed, *the most perfect kind of understanding obtainable.* Contradictions are ordinarily rejected by us because of their failure to express any rational thought, but this characteristic they of course also share with enlightenment, for enlightenment too does not express any rational thought. This is why Buddhism, with its doctrine of the Middle Way, has been undeterred by contradictions. This may be illustrated by a tale told in a sutra by the Buddha himself:

> A man traveling across a field encountered a tiger. He fled, the tiger after him. Coming to a precipice, he caught hold of the root of a wild vine and swung himself down over the edge. The tiger sniffed at him from above. Trembling, the man looked down to where, far below, another tiger was waiting to eat him. Only the vine sustained him.
>
> Two mice, one white and one black, little by little started to gnaw away the vine. The man saw a luscious strawberry near him. Grasping the vine with one hand, he plucked the strawberry with the other. How sweet it tasted!
>
> *The Gospel According to Zen*

First of all, this is a parable, an example of wisdom; but what does it really mean? The two tigers represent the worry or anxiety of any conceptual conflict: the thought that p, versus the thought that $not\text{-}p$, for any proposition, p. However, the man cannot maintain these two contradictory thoughts forever:

sooner or later the binary logic of true/false, represented by the two mice gnawing at his indecision, will force him to choose between p, $not\text{-}p$. In this state, man does not feel integrated or whole, he is disintegrating with indecision; his spiritual 'death' is symbolized in this parable by his impending physical death. To see how salvation (as represented by the strawberry) may yet be possible let us apply this sutra to real life, perhaps to the young man described by Sartre.

In Sartre's example, the man has two choices: whether to stay and care for his mother, or whether to travel and join the Free French. These are his two tigers: the option of going to fight is the tiger of not caring for his mother; the option of caring for his mother is the tiger of not going to fight. Each of these tigers threatens pain: the mental pain of guilt. In his conflict he is hanging from a vine, with 'no way of judging', as Sartre puts it. This situation persists as long as he continues to perceive his circumstances in this rigid way. But when he allows himself to mentally transcend this view he suddenly becomes able to perceive the strawberry, which has been in front of him the whole time; its delicious flavour symbolizes the joy and freedom of transcendence.

On my account, this transcendence signals the possibility of conceptual change. Thus, the experience symbolized by tasting the strawberry may have practical value, providing a 'Middle Way' between the two tigers. For we have seen that there are other options for Sartre's pupil which can combine caring for his mother with supporting the resistance. He is blind to these other options because both he and Sartre believe the decision can only be a responsible one if it is the expression of a clear thought. But an action can only be conceived in thought if we possess the relevant concepts. In this example, it seems he has no clear concept of an action that is *intermediate between* caring for his mother and fighting with the resistance, and so this is not an action he feels he can responsibly choose. In order to find this middle way, the pupil needed to allow himself to taste the delicious strawberry, i.e. he needed to allow himself to transcend his conflicting thoughts so as to reconceptualize them – precisely what Sartre interprets as irresponsible.

For, as we have just seen, enlightenment only comes by surrendering the will. Indeed, we may even surely say that the Buddha himself, as the basis of his own teaching, originally proposed his Middle Way of No-I, to avoid choosing between the existence and the nonexistence of a self. In doing this, the Buddha's response to the choice being offered was to reject the choice, and I believe this is also what he is recommending, for life in general, with the sutra about the tigers. For this parable seems to be hinting that the strategy of rejecting a dichotomy, which the Buddha used for the self, may be capable of more extensive application. It seems to me the sutra is suggesting that, for any mental conflict we experience, the mental state of enlightenment or nirvana can enable us to devise a 'middle way' between the contradictory options. In this way we can see the existence of a mode of understanding beyond contradictions to have been part of the Buddha's original message.

This sutra also demonstrates in particular how the Buddha saw mental conflicts as the cause of much of our suffering, and how enlightenment is what in life enables us to steer a middle course between such contradictory options. In this way, enlightenment provides the meaning of life. But what makes the Buddha's teaching work in practice, why is it that transcending our processes of thought and perception produce genuine enlightenment, in the sense that it succeeds in revealing to us a practical path through life? Buddhism does not say. In the present work, I have endeavoured to provide a cognitive theory as to how this mental transcendence may be the elevation to consciousness of our hidden cognitive processes of conceptual change. However, even within this theory, these processes of course are experienced non-conceptually, and so enlightenment remains mystical. For, while particular current intuitions might well be explicable in thought by reference to particular future concepts, there are no concepts which can in general explain *all* intuitions past, present and future. Hence intuition is not conceivable in thought.

Consequently, both Hinduism and Buddhism recognize that our thinking and perceptual processes need to be temporarily disabled, if we are to see past them to the ultimate nature of reality, and the meaning of life. To this end, they both recognize contradictions as having positive value, as is clear both from Kena and from the above parable. It seems indeed that transcendence is nothing less than a state of receptivity to contradictions. Thus a prevailing grasp of contradictions, far from being foreign to human nature, indicates rather that we are in touch with who we really are, and where we are going in life. It appears to do this by liberating us from the repressive strictures of conceptual thought. Our will, being conceptual, now becomes subordinate to mystical insight, or intuition, instead of dominating it.

This is the nature of the change brought by enlightenment, and why enlightenment can only be achieved by a form of surrender. As we come to study the Mahayana and Zen, we shall see that in Buddhism such concepts as No-I, satori, sunyata etc. seem to be best interpreted as describing one's state of mind when grasping contradictions, for that is really what is meant by saying these concepts are indescribable. This, I have argued, is experienced on particular occasions as ahas, or intuitions of specific future meanings; it is the recognition of a local ambiguity in which some of the given words or signs are seen as potentially reinterpretable. More generally, it is a state expressing a readiness to loosen our rigid interpretations of signs, in preparation for wit, wisdom or conceptual change. But if this cognitive account is to yield a valid description of Buddhist enlightenment, it can only be if the relevant receptivity or readiness is permanent and life-changing, and not just confined to one or two special occasions. In other words, the nature and value of transcendence must be understood in its fullest generality, and not just confined to particular parables or wise judgements.

And of course if this universality is understood, it must not be understood in words alone; it cannot simply be the thought that often in life we can understand contradictions by a non-conceptual process, or something of the sort. For, merely believing philosophical thoughts without possessing the corresponding mystical insight we already know to be insufficient for enlightenment. This was evident in the Buddha's message from the start, for otherwise enlightenment would have been expressible in thought. Such an intellectual process is the very opposite of what has been meant by enlightenment. Rather, we mean a permanent mental change in a person whereby they are now able to habitually enact exactly what may have been said by just such an intellectual description.

This means that enlightenment or redemption furnishes a life-skill: it enables a permanent commitment to making transcendence one's number one priority at all times, and always making conceptual thought subservient to this. We can perhaps refer to this ultimate decision as *the Existential Choice*, for it really is the ultimate decision, the choice of choices. And this existential choice is surely a reversal or overthrow of the normal priorities of most of us most of the time. For, more than the transcendence of thought, mostly what we more specifically care about is our family, our career or our religion, in short our human relationships, or else our abstract principles and theories (such as existentialism, or Buddhism itself); and all of these are of course known to us and cherished by conceptual thought.

But enlightenment is not any of these, nor is it information about any state of affairs; it is a skill: it is knowing how to live. Enlightenment describes a clear understanding of the universal role that transcending our thoughts has in guiding us through life. It is not the mastery of any theory, not even the theory of

Buddhism or of cognition. Rather, it means forming a new relationship with your own concepts, learning to use your mind in a wholly new way about whatever it chances to encounter. This is, for instance, more than merely becoming more open-minded, for that is just being open to thinking new thoughts with the concepts we already have; whereas enlightenment is being open to the possibility of entirely new concepts. However, it is clear that doing all this unconsciously would not be enlightenment either, and so enlightenment must also include a full awareness of the nature and operation of this new skill, without necessarily being able to have any abstract thoughts about it. Only this is understanding the meaning of life.

But what kind of understanding can this possibly be? It is an understanding of the scope and limits of conceptual thought *in general*, yet without thinking about conceptual thought. What is being envisaged here is the possibility of an understanding as abstract and general as logic itself, but without being logic. For we are referring to those anti-logical *movements of the mind*, common to all the practical examples we have considered so far, of friendship, maternal love, sovereignty etc. grasped in pure abstraction from them all, and yet *without the use of concepts*. Indeed, we might describe enlightenment as the grasp of a new creative kind of inference, which is anti-logical in the sense that it graciously accepts contradictions from which to infer new meanings. Unlike logic, such inferences cannot be defined by any rules, but, like logic, it is a mental skill acting upon our thoughts which, as Lewis Carroll's tortoise demonstrated for logic, need not itself consist in the thinking of any thought (Chapter 5). Enlightenment may indeed be to experience the very balance of the mind itself, in its tranquil readiness to weigh the contrary claims of competing thoughts. Thus, we learn to judge our thoughts instead of merely thinking them.

It is surely only such a fundamental change in our relationship with our own thoughts that can inaugurate a fundamental change in our lives. Where before we may have despised our own contradictory nature, now we may come to embrace it as the key to our higher being. This we may also recognize as learning to love oneself; it is the basis of self-esteem. To transcend *all* our concepts is to no longer allow oneself to be judged ultimately by any of them, nor by any ideas or principles or relationships 'pressing down' on us. For one's inner identity or sense of self is greater than them all, since these external standards are all constrained by logic, but our innermost self is not. In other words, enlightenment can put an end to depression, replacing it by mystic insight. Not only does this dispel the suffering from what Sartre called 'bad faith' due to stereotypes and self-images of every kind, it also dispels the suffering imposed by any concept of oneself whatsoever, including Sartre's own notion of 'authenticity', since all such concepts are mistaken. Hence the 'anguish' of Sartre's 'freedom' evaporates since, in reality, this freedom was only ever the repression of our capacity for transcendence, by tying us down to whatever particular concepts the mind currently contained.

Nagarjuna, master of contradictions

In this way, the Buddha, by introducing the experience of enlightenment, had tried to emancipate us from fixed concepts about ourselves. Nevertheless, predictably, a huge body of Buddhist scriptures, the *Abhidharma*, developed, conceptually analysing the very experiences of perception, enlightenment, the nature of self etc. In so doing, they were attempting to 'clarify' in concepts the Buddha's teaching which, I have argued, was implicitly about the transcendence of all such concepts. It was in response to this that, in south India, the great Buddhist sage Nagarjuna (200 AD), viewed by many Buddhists as second only to the Buddha himself, wrote a work redirecting Buddhism back to its roots. He did this by developing the critique of the limits of conceptual thought, that had always been implicit in the need for enlightenment to be inexpressible, but which had never been made explicitly by the Buddha, and had subsequently become obscured.

In the Madhyamaka,[1] Nagarjuna courageously subjected nearly every concept central to Buddhism to the same treatment the Buddha had applied to 'Self' by exposing its internal contradictions (Chapter 3). But far from being a bad thing, such contradictions are, to Nagarjuna, all to the good in helping us to see that it is only in contradictions that true wisdom is to be found. In order to examine this Nagarjuna method in more detail, let us now consider just one out of the hundreds of verses (called tetralemmas) making up his Madhyamaka:

Error does not develop
In one who is in error.
Error does not develop
In one who is not in error.

This paradox appears to exhaust all the possibilities: either a person is in error or she is not in error; hence it is apparently not possible to ever fall into error. However, that would be contrary to ordinary or conventional speech, which Nagarjuna wishes to defend. Rather, the targets of this contradiction were his fellow Buddhist scholars, who taught that all the significant errors in life are ultimately due to being in a fundamental spiritual state of error (such as, for example, believing that a personal self exists). It is the inadequacy of this 'ultimate' speech which Nagarjuna wants to expose.

His purpose with such verses was not to provide better versions of the prevailing ultimate or spiritual terms, but to show in general that really all such terms are self-contradictory, demonstrating that ultimate speech can never provide perfect wisdom, but that the entire enterprise is flawed. Thus, in the above verse, Nagarjuna is not attempting to communicate an improved concept of error, as we have been doing throughout this work for the practical concepts: friendship, maternal love, sovereignty etc. earlier. *No aha moment is being attempted,* only a contradiction. Rather, his aim seems to have been something different: exposing the contradictory nature of any such ultimate description; it is this which we are intended to understand as the hidden meaning of the verse. Moreover, he wished to demonstrate that this must be *essentially* the case, since all reality is ultimately self-contradictory, or 'empty'. Nagarjuna is thereby affirming the Buddha's belief that enlightenment must be indescribable by showing that any attempt to describe its insights results in contradiction. Hence, no language, however ultimate, can ever be adequate to describe reality.

To see, for instance, why no ultimate or spiritual concept of Error can be consistent, consider the verse cited. It is impossible for such spiritual errors to be due solely to a state of error, says Nagarjuna, by considering the logical alternatives. Either one is currently in spiritual error or one is currently not in spiritual error; the question is, how does error ever get started, how does spiritual error come into being? If we take the first case, a person already in the state of error, then error cannot develop here because it already exists in this person. On the other hand, consider a person not in this state of error; then the state of error could only develop in him if he commits some spiritual errors. But if there is no trace of spiritual error currently infecting him then what could cause him to commit an error? It is impossible since Error is the cause of all such errors. Thus the concept of the spiritual state of error is shown to be incoherent as an origin of all errors because it makes it impossible for this spiritual state to develop where it does not already exist. In many ways, this move by Nagarjuna resembles our modern Western rejection of those metaphysical terms which appear to use complex theories to hide logical inconsistencies. For we know in normal life that well-intentioned people can and do fall into moral and spiritual error; hence the spiritual concept of Error is, as Nagarjuna would say, 'imperfect'.

So far, this resembles the kind of inference noted in our earlier paradoxes about various naturalistic concepts. From an apparent contradiction, instead of inferring that one or other of the premises is false, we are instead rejecting the inconsistent concept itself. However, there the similarity ends, because no perfected concept of error is being hinted at. Rather, it is simply being demonstrated that what is a familiar Buddhist concept must, strictly speaking, be inexpressible in any language, ultimate or otherwise; and this itself is the primary meaning of the verse. For it seems the reason Nagarjuna wrote the Madhyamaka is because he had discerned *in general* that the reason we invent such idealized or 'ultimate' concepts is exactly because they cannot be comprehended by the mind as ordinary concepts. This, in turn, is reflected by the fact that, whenever we do try to comprehend the insights of enlightenment with the mind by ordinary concepts, we end up contradicting ourselves. It is to avoid this fate that we appear to be tempted to replace them by 'ultimate' concepts. But this is a false move, Nagarjuna seems to be telling us, for the same fate befalls the ultimate language also, since any language, even an ultimate language, has to be self-consistent. Rather, we should simply face the fact that every language attempting to describe these matters becomes inconsistent, and instead perfect our understanding by attempting to grasp the implications of the contradictions themselves.

This at first sight may seem rather odd: how does one perfect a concept or belief by showing it to be full of contradictions? But let us recall the original concept of a Middle Way; Buddhism had always wanted to eliminate that ultimate speech which employed an idea of the Self, while nevertheless elevating the perfectly serviceable idea of the self in conventional speech: a middle way. The Middle Way, by holding in mind at the same time two contradictory uses of a word, really endorses that special form of understanding which I have tried to convey through poetry, paradox, and practical wisdom.

For Nagarjuna had seen that if the Middle Way could be used to 'perfect' the supposed concept of the self (by showing it to be inexpressible) so equally could it be used to perfect *every Buddhist concept whatsoever*: action, perception, suffering, even nirvana itself. For example, his tetralemma enables us to understand Error in both its aspects, the spiritual and the conventional at the same time. And, as with 'Self' (but unlike our earlier naturalistic concepts) the contradiction is here intended to demonstrate how *inexpressibility is a vital aspect of all such spiritual concepts*, i.e. they cannot be expressed in any speech, ultimate or otherwise. In the case of our earlier naturalistic concepts, understanding was achieved by (the prospect of) eliminating the contradiction. Here, however, there is no such prospect, and understanding consists in grasping the *permanence* of the contradiction, and its necessity. By presenting his ideas in this way, Nagarjuna aims, not to replace, for example, the metaphysical concept of Error by the conventional one, but to enhance ('perfect') our understanding by showing that Error is not a concept at all. Any revised understanding of Error as a psychological state would, in order to articulate Nagarjuna's intention, have to present it as *indefinable in concepts*, and only intelligible by enlightenment. It seems, for Nagarjuna, that conventional concepts may, like the practical concepts discussed by me earlier, sometimes be logically consistent. But if there is any such spiritual or ultimate 'concept' (like Error) then it appears that it can only be understood, like enlightenment itself, by grasping the various contradictions to which it is subject, and seeing the necessity and relevance of these, and their inevitability.

In this way, Nagarjuna's contradiction destroys the illusion that Error might be expressible without the use of contradictions in a pure, ultimate speech of some kind. The Buddha had surely seen how our knowledge of an ultimate concept of the Self or

Atman can lead to contradictions (Chapter 3). Moreover, that these can be avoided by experiencing such self-knowledge as real but inexpressible in language or thought, i.e. by experiencing enlightenment. In a similar fashion, Nagarjuna has now shown how supposed spiritual states such as Error must equally lead to contradictions. These too can only be avoided by understanding each such spiritual state in the Madhyamaka, not by means of ultimate concepts, nor even by any concepts at all, but as being inexpressible or 'empty'. For each spiritual state X, its contradictions prompt a revised 'empty' concept of X, in which it is understood that the 'concept' of X can only be grasped by understanding how it contradicts itself, as shown by the various tetralemmas for X. It is this that reveals X to be inexpressible (empty).

Since it contrasts ultimate with conventional speech, this approach was evidently based upon a renewed respect for the use of ordinary language ('conventional speech') in which we regularly speak, for instance, not only of knowing oneself, but also of making errors. Thus in the above example, Error in ultimate speech (which is 'eternal') is being rejected by means of error in conventional speech (which can develop in time). But the ultimate concept, instead of now being eliminated, is rather retained, and indeed may be said to be *transcended* by means of the contradiction. For, an understanding conferred by contradiction transcends every concept, no matter how ultimate, and is also the understanding conferred by enlightenment. Contrary to Western analytic philosophy, there is a recognition that, because of its ability to do this, sometimes contradiction can itself be something of inestimable value.

And so we can see that Nagarjuna, with his gnomic utterances and cryptic exercises in dialectic, was performing the service of restoring the purity of the Buddha's original vision of a Middle Way by extending it from the self alone to the whole of Buddhism. In place of the various concepts of the Abhidharma,

Nagarjuna, in virtue of the inconsistencies he demonstrated, spoke of all these instead as modes of *sunyata* or emptiness. Inevitably, there has been a resulting tendency to think of this emptiness itself as just another ultimate concept, in the same way as Self or Error, namely: as a super-abstract 'Void' emptier than any void previously conceived. Nagarjuna warns against this tendency and, in a move that is often particularly baffling to modern Western minds, makes the pronouncement that even descriptions of emptiness are empty. By this he merely meant that if emptiness is treated (mistakenly) as another ultimate concept, then it would have to be as self-contradictory as every other 'ultimate' concept.

However, from the tetralemmas, we can surely now see that emptiness best describes, not anything of which we can conceive, but only *the kind of understanding we acquire from contradictions*. It is unfortunate, however, that Nagarjuna only felt able to articulate the content of this understanding via the same mode of expression as his predecessors, namely by devising an ultimate concept 'emptiness' by which to describe it. For it is clear that his real meaning for each ultimate concept X was given only by understanding the contradictions implied by X, i.e. only by the transcending of those concepts, and never by ascribing yet another concept 'empty' to them. It is only these contradictions that define the emptiness of X. However, one result has been inevitably that emptiness has been mistakenly venerated by some as a new supreme concept to live by.

Zen Buddhism

A new variant of Mahayana Buddhism subsequently developed in India from this concept of emptiness. Around 500 AD a travelling monk, Bodhidharma, brought the Mahayana to China, where it evolved into a new kind of Buddhism known as *Chan*, transferring to Japan as Zen. Initially, according to Suzuki, Zen enlightenment was viewed as a gradual process, culminating in the view of Shen-hsiu of the emptiness of the mind as a bright mirror, where the aim of meditation is to keep wiping the mirror free of dust. However, if the dust is conceptual thought, then if it is completely eliminated how can the mirror retain any relevance to life? As Suzuki says, meditation then becomes just self-serving, and has little more than a tranquilizing effect on the mind. The reader may note additionally that, in the cognitive theory being developed here, a primary function of transcendence is to create new concepts; in this case, the very purpose of the mirror would then be to create more dust, and so comparison with the Zen of Shen-hsiu appears to break down.

However, around the same time, 700 AD, the sixth patriarch of Zen, Hui-neng, became 'vehemently' opposed to this view, and Suzuki reports him as objecting that: 'Since all is empty, where can the dust alight?' In other words, there is no separate mirror. Hui-neng further realized that since the source of this emptiness is logical contradiction, then it cannot be said to arise gradually. It was on this basis that Hui-neng introduced the notion of enlightenment as a sudden event, providing us with the version of Zen that we have today. He and his followers resorted to unpredictable behaviour or self-contradictory statements (such as 'the sound of one hand clapping') in order to provoke an understanding beyond words. The intention is that, after the mind has been thoroughly prepared by meditation and study, it may take only a small impulse to effect a cataclysmic change in our consciousness, a mystical experience known as satori.

It is for this reason that, thereafter, one school of Zen employed only koans such as 'look at the North Star by turning around towards the south', in order to induce satori. What is the purpose of such koans? The aim is to understand that emptiness is at the heart of everything; thus, for example, we do not experience a higher or spiritual self, since this leads to contradictions. Nevertheless, we do possess such a sense of self of which we have no concept; so Zen refers to this as No-Self, signifying the emptiness at its core. This is another way of saying we only understand it by understanding how we understand contradictions – which is a completely new way of understanding.

Nagarjuna had shown how this could be done with all spiritual concepts: mind, freedom, error... and Zen now introduces a series of variants No-Mind, No-Freedom, No-Error... to indicate the contradictory (empty) nature of each one.[2] For example spiritual freedom is not actually a feeling we can experience, but we may nevertheless possess a 'sense' of freedom. It is also, of course, a disposition to act in new and original ways, but the inner sense of spiritual freedom generating these meaningful new ways of acting is inexpressible. And this, we have now learnt, means it can only be expressed by self-contradiction – which we can perhaps signify by 'No-Freedom'. Similarly with spiritual error, and all the other spiritual concepts. And so Zen requires monks to concentrate on a self-contradictory koan to generate this insight.

The Chinese for No- or none is *wu*, and sometimes monks were simply asked to contemplate the word *wu*, signifying emptiness itself. Concerning the genesis of satori, Suzuki[3] quotes a Zen master as saying:

Do not waste your time by merely thinking of '*Wu*' as if you were no more than a simpleton, make no attempt to give a false solution to it by means of speculation and imagination. Resolutely put yourself, heart and soul, into unravelling the problem of '*Wu*'! When suddenly, as you let go of your hold, there comes a grand overturning of the whole system of consciousness, and for the first time you realize in a most luminous manner what all this finally comes to.

By concentrating purely on '*Wu*' the resulting mystical experience is intended to give insight into all the '*Wu*' concepts. More generally, by focusing on a contradiction, the experience of satori is intended to bring insight into the contradictory nature of all the No-concepts. We see, moreover, that the author is not advocating tranquil meditation, but on the contrary the solving of a problem; requiring what Suzuki mildly calls: 'the spirit of inquiry'. The monk is actually enjoined to take his koan everywhere and to think of his koan day and night, until he has solved it. Far from tranquillity, the koan method is intended to induce a conflict in the mind of the seeker between his imagined need for conceptual understanding of the koan, and his knowledge, from its contradictory nature, that this is impossible. Only his passionate desire to understand will bring on the necessary crisis: leading to satori. The Zen master Hakuin has described this as: 'something akin to an explosion, as if an ice basin were shattered into pieces, or as if a tower of jade had crumbled, and the event is accompanied by a feeling of immense joy such as never before has been experienced in their lives.'

This is because Satori grasps, not just how the particular contradiction of one koan demonstrates the emptiness of that particular concept, but rather shows, via this koan, how contradictions in general show the emptiness of reality in general. This is quite an achievement; Nagarjuna had shown, case by case, how contradiction is at the heart of each ultimate concept, but it is less clear that this must also be true of ordinary concepts that we think with every day. For it was necessary to grasp, in a leap of insight, not only the contradiction of a particular koan, and its link to its own concepts, but to grasp the link between (meaningful) contradictions in general, and the concepts of which they are composed. Nevertheless, it is remarkable that Zen discovered this non-logical significance of contradictions in general, without possessing any abstract symbolism by which to express it in general terms. For example Suzuki himself remarks, 'The Zen experience evidently opens a closed door revealing all the treasures behind it. It suddenly leaps over to the other side of logic and starts a dialectics of its own.'

We now consider further the possible connection between the Zen experience and the mystical theory of cognition I began to develop in earlier chapters. In the following narrative we see how Zen does indeed hint also at the transcendence of ordinary concepts:

> One evening Doken despairingly implored his friend to assist him in the solution of the mystery of life. The friend said, 'I am willing to help you in every way I can, but there are some things in which I cannot be of any help to you; these you must look after for yourself.' Doken expressed the desire to know what these things were. Said his friend: 'For instance when you are hungry or thirsty, my eating of food or drinking will not fill your stomach; you must eat and drink for yourself. When you want to respond to the calls of nature you must take care of yourself, for I cannot be of any use to you. And then it is you and nobody else that will carry your body along this highway.' This friendly counsel at once opened the mind of the truth-seeking monk, who was so transported with his discovery that he did not know how to express his joy.
>
> DT Suzuki, in *The Gospel According to Zen*

This narrative becomes clearer if, instead of activities of the body, we consider those of the mind. For although information, like food and drink, can be given to us, satori cannot be given to us, but is our knowledge of how to transcend our information. This, at last, is a reply that might also assist the tramp at the information desk. For, in the same spirit, Doken's friend might equally have said that he, Doken, can be told a joke, and even have it explained to him, but only Doken himself can laugh at it. Earlier, we said transcending information means being receptive to a contradiction so as to reinterpret some of its terms, with the possibility of creating new meaning. This shows us the link between Doken and our ongoing cognitive preoccupation with contradictions. Information consists only in fixed meanings which may conflict; but two people like Doken and his friend, or like the tramp and the clerk, treating that same conflict as poetry or paradox by transcending it, may equally be engaged in a shared form of communication – by dialectic. Furthermore, I am now suggesting that our sudden understanding of this cognitive truth in its fullest generality may be tantamount to satori. In that case an aha moment, instead of merely registering a joke say, might possess universality: for it might be a flash of insight, satori, that is life-changing – providing insight, not into this or that situation, but into situations in general, and our general response to them.

Consequently, it seems to follow that our earlier cognitive appreciation of naturalistic contradictions can now be affirmed with a universality equal to that of Zen. Then, by using the modern resources of symbolic logic to express that universality, the spiritual significance of contradictions can be defined more precisely. The logical analysis of thoughts outlined in Chapter 4 can for this purpose be formalized even further by saying that the simplest thoughts p comprise a concept F ascribed to objects a, which we might represent by the formula, $F(a)$. All other thoughts are expressed by logical combinations of such simple formulas. Now consider any pair of simple or complex contradictory thoughts p, q where q entails *not-p* because some concept F is being ascribed to an object a, by p, but being denied of the same object a, by q. Then we have seen how in cases of paradox or practical wisdom it is sometimes possible to reinterpret the meanings of some of the *occurrences* of F as $F1$ (say, those in p) differently from others $F2$ (say those in q), so that p, q no longer contradict.

For example, recall (Chapter 8) the commanding heights x of Ateb conquered by Aphla, and the contradiction as to whether x belongs to Aphla or x belongs to Ateb. In the above symbolism, let p = x *belongs to Aphla*, and let q = x *belongs to Ateb*, and let F = x *belongs to*. Then, clearly, F is being ascribed to Aphla by p, but being denied of Aphla by q.

Then recall that this contradiction of p, q was resolved by the diplomat by altering the meaning of x *belongs to* differently in each of p and q. For in p he reinterpreted it to mean 'x belongs militarily to', and in q he reinterpreted it to mean 'x belongs socio-economically to'. This new analysis by the diplomat brought peace to the region because it was acceptable to both combatants.

It is not such precise thoughts, however, that we call *understanding the contradiction*, for no contradiction expresses a precise thought. Furthermore, the diplomat probably did not immediately think of this resolution in its final form; his prescience rather consisted in an intuition in which he conceived that the unitary concept '*belongs*' can be split into two kinds, *belongs-1* and *belongs-2*, without being able to say fully what each one of these means. It is this earlier stage of intuition during which the final resolution was merely glimpsed as a possibility or prospect which we more justifiably call understanding the contradiction. At this stage, p, q are grasped purely abstractly as a partially interpreted pair of logical forms, x *belongs-1 to Aphla*, and x *belongs-2 to Ateb* respectively, without fully interpreting either form. And perhaps it is the formal anticipation of such possible ambiguities in general which we are now recognizing as the content of an ongoing state of *transcendence*. For we have described transcendence as a state of balance, or ongoing receptivity to contradictions.

I am suggesting that it is something of this kind, universalized to the whole of reality (and perhaps symbolized as above) which characterizes the Zen understanding of contradictory koans. Or rather, which characterizes the Zen understanding of the contradictory or empty nature of reality. If so, then it seems the symbolic formalism of logic in Western analytic philosophy has relevance to the enigmatic pronouncements of Zen, and vice versa. For, instead of referring just to one particular situation, satori is said to be a flash of insight into the very nature of reality in general. What might be meant by this? Well, we might say that where some movement of the mind, such as an aha (or a logical inference), has repetitive or even universal presence during various different cases of cognition, then we might begin to say such moves are necessary to cognition itself, to our knowledge of reality. This then is an *epistemological* statement about the logical nature of knowledge.

But again, if these mental moves are indeed necessary to all possible knowledge, so that knowledge is scarcely possible without them, then also this might be good grounds for suggesting the *metaphysical* view that these moves are necessary to our very concept of reality; that perhaps they define part of the nature of reality itself. This would be because whatever cannot be known without these moves could hardly be said to be real. If contradictions can in some general way provide insight into new meaning, then this would surely mean that facts themselves are not rigidly defined (as in Wittgenstein's *Tractatus*), since the concepts of which they are composed are not rigidly defined. Instead of objects being related by fixed concepts, our concepts may, on the contrary, be flexible and slowly evolving as a result of contradictions, with only the transcendence of these contradictions being fixed and eternal. It might even be said, in such a case, that all concepts are merely temporary, and that contradiction (emptiness) is the only permanent feature of reality.

If this is the meaning of Zen, then it is remarkable that, lacking the techniques of Western analytic philosophy, i.e. without any general theory of concepts, or formal symbolism for logic, Zen nevertheless came to recognize the nature and significance of contradictions and our mental capacity to understand them, together with an appreciation that ordinary conceptual thought lacks this capacity. Inevitably, however, the exact nature of the link between ordinary life and the contradictory status of satori has remained obscure. Nevertheless, as Suzuki said, such a link must exist; otherwise satori would not have the relevance to life that it does. We have all along been investigating this relevance, but we shall now consider it further.

Chapter 10

The Fall and Redemption of Man

We have seen how, after special mental preparation for this very thing, a life-changing mystical experience may be possible that is known, in various traditions, as redemption, salvation or enlightenment. The vital consequence of this experience, apart from its ecstatic nature, is that it confers genuine understanding, enabling us to live a more fulfilling life, by making better decisions and resolving many of the dilemmas that confront us.

This then is enlightenment. But is it possible to be enlightened naturally, without undergoing any such gruelling conversion process? Indeed by good parenting and a favourable culture, we may believe so. However, while this may routinely lead to fairly contented living, it may not necessarily produce any clear insight into the nature of life in general. Recalling for example Tolstoy's observation of his serfs (Chapter 2), he noted that they appeared to know how to act in life and were not troubled by the sophisticated doubts that afflicted him. By a sort of folk wisdom they were often able to, as we may say, 'instinctively' make the right judgements, naturally putting intuition before calculation. In other words, they were perhaps habitually able to transcend dilemmas so as to choose, in particular cases, a middle way, without having any generalized understanding of how they do so. Perhaps such priorities are innate in us and we tend to trust them naturally, providing they have not been drilled out of us. But even if this is the case, our grasp of them will be at best patchy and prone to error. The beliefs of Tolstoy's serfs were produced not only by intuition, but by 'the grossest superstition' and also by the teachings of the Russian Orthodox Church, and it is unclear in any given problem in life which of these would prevail, i.e. whether intuition would always be accorded the ultimate priority.

Religion is neither necessary nor sufficient for this mystical commitment to the non-conceptual. Neither is this wisdom, this secret, merely one of learning to emulate instinctual animal behaviour, learning to just act 'naturally'. On the contrary, it is a highly sophisticated insight privy only to beings who can think, and who are consequently familiar with the limitations of thinking. But this insight into the limits of thinking is not guaranteed because to every thinker: the insight *is not itself a case of thinking*. All that can be guaranteed by ordinary familiarity with thinking is some facility at thinking itself. But appreciation of the limitations of thinking is hard-won and by no means guaranteed. For it seems there is nothing in thinking itself that tells us what it is that thinking cannot accomplish.

The Existential Choice

And so it seems that for the finest kind of life, to live out life to its fullest expectancy, it is necessary to be fully conscious of the limits to our thoughts and actions, as well as what they are capable of. This includes a grasp of our actions, not only by conceptual thought, but by intuition. And to grasp this with maximum generality, i.e. to grasp life as a whole, it is necessary to comprehend how our thoughts must, in general, be subservient to the transcendence of thought, and to adopt this as a conscious choice. Making this decision is the ultimate act of faith, and is what we have called the Existential Choice, for it is a choice which must be constantly renewed and used to guide *all* our decisions in life. Only in this way can enlightenment be said to have been achieved, and it is clear that such a universal priority as this cannot simply be instinctive or acquired by habit, but requires a unique kind of understanding.

The Existential Choice is thus not the same as enlightenment, but rather is the way we make use of enlightenment thereafter; it expresses our commitment to what we have understood during the mystical experience of enlightenment. What we have understood, of course, cannot be put into words, and so this raises the question: how can what I have grasped be said to possess full universality, not just particular to the occasion that evoked it, but applying to all situations in life, if it does not consist of generalized thoughts? In this regard it will be helpful to recall the actions of the Zen swordsman (Chapter 2).

We saw that the Zen sword stroke, while voluntary, is not conceptual, i.e. is not the execution of any thought, for recall that the swordsman was 'purposeless and egoless'. Therefore the sword stroke was not an act of will, since for every such act we must will p, where p is a thought, i.e. a state of affairs to be brought about. It was for this reason that, in the midst of all this dynamic activity, we thought of the sword stroke as being passive despite being voluntary, or unopposed. Now, in a related but non-physical fashion, speaking purely of the mind, notice that we similarly refer to our commitment to transcendence, paradoxically, as an act of surrender. We may thus say that choosing to transcend our own thoughts is, like the sword stroke, also purposeless and egoless. The reason is that the acts chosen by such a commitment are not conceptual: there are no alternatives not-p which we are rejecting since, when acting from transcendence, there are no thoughts p which we are willing. Rather, our actions are now the outcomes of transcendence directly, without any mediating thoughts. And since transcendence is our higher identity, our sense of self, we might identify such spiritually motivated actions as acts of pure self-expression, unwilled and unplanned.

But while this may be the case for specific expressions of transcendence, specific choices, it may be believed that in order to make the Existential Choice itself, i.e. to prioritize transcendence in general, the use of a general thought p is unavoidable, for this supreme decision cannot be understood in any other way. However, I have proposed (Chapter 9) that it may be possible for a mystical experience to be perfectly general, not just confined to one situation but applying to all possible situations, yet not require the comprehension of any defining characteristic. For example, just as a particular type of physical movement can be comprehended purely as a skill, so it was suggested that the transcending of thoughts might be grasped purely as a movement of the mind, as a way of relating to our thoughts, without itself being the occurrence of any thought. And this mental skill might be something I feel able to commit myself to, despite lacking any concept of what it is, hence without it being an act of will.

This is certainly paradoxical, and may seem to be impossible: how can something so insightful, such a deep act of understanding, be rated merely as a mental skill? Even if this is the case, the decisions to invoke the use of a skill would seem to require a form of understanding other than the skill itself if it is to be voluntary, and not mere habit. It might seem that, in order to properly understand the nature of enlightenment and how to benefit by putting it into practice, I may need also to possess the *concept* of enlightenment. For it now seems that only by thinking about the transcendence of thought in general could I coherently ensure that my thoughts will always in future be subordinated to my transcendence of them. In other words, apart from such thought, how else is my commitment to transcendence to acquire universality? This would seem to require each pair of conflicting thoughts to be understood not as themselves alone, but only as instances of a prior concept of conflict or contradiction in general.

But if so, then this would appear to deny not only what we have previously said about enlightenment (Chapter 9), but also the claim being made by Zen for the experience of satori. For, in a suitably prepared mind, Zen requires only one singular experience to awaken the mind to a realm of possibilities, affecting the whole of life. And this of course is to be accomplished without the employment of any conceptual thought. It seems that by grasping just one contradiction, expressed as the meaning of a single koan, we are thereby enabled to see what is involved in grasping *every* (meaningful) contradiction, and in this way our insight achieves generality. Perhaps the aim of the koan is not to convey one particular meaning, but to demonstrate an entirely new mode of mental functioning. In the present work, I too have used relatively few examples to convey what I mean, and yet these exemplars may have perhaps likewise been adequate to demonstrate a means to understand contradictions in general.

Like Zen practitioners, we may thus be enabled to grasp, purely by inner exemplars, the sharp contrast between thought and its transcendence without possessing any general conceptual understanding of it. If so, then surely this experience may suffice for me to commit myself to this generalized distinction, still without employing conceptual thought, so as to *prioritize* one aspect of the experience, transcendence, over the other, thought, in general. This then would be the Existential Choice, undertaken non-conceptually, without the employment of conceptual thought. One consequence of this would appear to be that not only is understanding possible without the use of concepts, but also *choices* are possible without the use of concepts. This difference is expressed by transcendence and by our commitment to transcendence, respectively.

It is spiritual freedom that allows us to choose actions non-conceptually, by means of transcendence, or self-awareness. However, in also saying we are responding *passively* to transcendence, it is easy to slip into believing that transcendence is the perception of a being such as the soul or higher self, which we have to conform to, making us appear to be unfree. But perhaps it is at this point that we should remind ourselves that transcending our will need not mean we are conceiving instead some other 'spiritual' being having supreme authority. Rather this, more modestly, normally just describes seeking to find a middle way when confronting contradictory requirements. In that case, if such modest transcendence were nevertheless said to be due to our comprehending a spiritual being, it would, as we have seen, have to be *defined* as a being enabling us to balance (meaningful) contradictions. Consequently, such a spiritual or supernatural being as the soul or Self would be not merely an unjustified concept, but a concept *only describable by self-contradiction*. Thus it would not be a concept at all, since any such concept would be logically inconsistent. Perhaps the safest thing to say is that if transcendence or self-awareness is the perception of a being, that being must be dialectic itself, i.e. it is nothing more than our own faculty for understanding certain kinds of self-contradiction.

This enables us at last to resolve the dilemma presented earlier, in Chapter 3, in the Kena Upanishad, by the words: *That which is not comprehended by the mind, but by which the mind comprehends, know that to be Brahman*. For, if by the mind is meant logical thought, then clearly contradictions are not comprehended by the mind. Nevertheless, since, on my analysis, certain contradictions can give rise to new concepts, and since the mind needs concepts in order to comprehend anything then, ironically, it is possible for contradictions to be that by means of which the mind comprehends (by creating its concepts), despite not themselves being comprehensible by the mind. In other words, it seems that (meaningful) contradictions themselves satisfy the requirements of the Kena narrative cited above. Therefore, contradictions may have been what Kena had been referring to all along. Nevertheless, Kena also equates this with our spiritual self, Brahman; and so, if this interpretation is correct, Brahman would then be a being definable only by contradictions, i.e. a self-contradictory being. Such a self-contradictory nature would indeed seem to provide the flexibility that at least some religions implicitly require 'spirit' to provide. Of course, no being can be that flexible without going out of existence. But only Buddhism appears to have taken the logical next step of acknowledging this by denying the existence of any such spirit. Contradictions are then confined just to the realm of human experience, rather than allowing them to define entities said to exist in the outside world.

Spiritual freedom vs free will

Divorced from its religious associations, the commitment to spiritual transcendence primarily concerns the experience of human freedom and creativity. In Sartre's example, it might describe how, when attempting to reconcile supporting the Free French with supporting his mother, the son might nevertheless be able to devise various actions that may not otherwise be intelligible to him in clear thoughts or plans. Nor would his actions then be motivated by religious faith, but purely by a creative impulse to produce a synthesis from the contradiction of a thesis and an antithesis. However, similar actions revealed to a religious person might equally be attributed, say, by a Hindu to the outcome of meditation, and by a Muslim or Christian to the outcome of prayer, rather than to their own creativity.

In all such cases, one common point of agreement might be that it would be inaccurate to say that the relevant actions are chosen by our free will, but rather that we were guided by something other than our own contrivance. Whatever the accompanying beliefs therefore we here refer to this transcendent response to the apparent contradictions in life as spiritual freedom. And spiritual freedom, being non-conceptual, is not at all the same thing as free will, since free will requires only concepts for its full expression, but spiritual freedom transcends the use of concepts. We may say perhaps that spiritual freedom employs a new kind of *intention*, other than the will, namely intuition, one example of which is the non-conceptual intention to dismantle apparent contraries, and to have faith that their parts can be recombined in a new and beneficial way. But, if so, such intuition seems to be a weaker or less strident kind of intention than the will; by comparison with the will, we have even been calling it 'passive', as it merely guides rather than determines our actions.

My thesis here is that any act of will is the choice to bring about some state of affairs p, conceivable in thought; hence free will is the freedom purely and simply to choose between such acts of will, i.e. the freedom to choose between acts p, q, r... conceived in thought by the agent. By contrast, a spiritual act is, in its very nature, not conceived in thought because it is normally aimed at eliminating a conflict in thought; it is a peace-making or reconciling act. Thus for example, doing one's duty can never be a perfectly spiritual act, since one's duty is always given by a rule preconceived in thought and hence requires an act of will. Consequently, a spiritual intention is a different kind of intention from an act of will, and spiritual freedom must be a different kind of freedom from free will. The implication of spiritual freedom in a given situation is that not only am I free to use my will to choose between all the p, q, r... that I can conceive, but that I am also free whether to employ my will *at all* (i.e. to employ my current concepts), or whether instead to transcend my will so as to seek out new concepts and a new understanding.

But there is a more fundamental decision, prior even to this, and that is the decision as to how I will live my life. For, in deciding *whether to be spiritually free* I make the Existential Choice, i.e. I decide whether to place free will or spiritual freedom in charge of my life. This ultimate choice cannot of course be itself the exercise of free will, because free will is always a decision between two different thoughts: doing p or not doing p, since acts of will are always conceptual. However, the Existential Choice itself, the decision as to whether thought or the transcending of thoughts is to be our top priority, cannot be a case of free will since one of the options, transcendence, need not be conceived in thought. Rather, this unique choice must itself be one of spiritual freedom. The fact is, the mind does not choose between the concept of the will and the *concept* of transcendence, as free will would require; it chooses only between *the use of the will* and *whether to transcend that use*. It chooses not between one concept and another but between acting in life purely so as to conform objects or people to clear concepts, or acting in life so as to sometimes balance contradictory concepts against each other, seeking a middle way, and not exclusively just pursue individual concepts via the will. This is a choice between two different mental activities: thinking and recognition, as the basis of our life.

The proof that this is not itself a conceptual decision is that there exist in the world millions of people who have attained wisdom, who have uncovered the secret of life, and yet who may not have within their minds any such *concept* as 'transcendence'; although transcendence is something they certainly do experience. Therefore, in choosing to put transcendence before thought such persons are not thinking thoughts about transcendence but, much like deciding to stand up or sit down, merely exercising a skill. Nor, as we have seen, need even an *enlightened* choice of transcendence, resulting from a mystical revelation, or require possession or acquisition of transcendence as a thinkable concept, in order for it to guide our life. In this case such a decision may, as assumed by Zen, be able to use the revelation itself as a life-altering exemplar.

However, if on the contrary the Existential Choice results in the negative decision to place the will firmly in charge, and allow transcendence only a scope determined by the will, i.e. by repressing and stifling transcendence, then this is nevertheless a spiritual choice (since what it is rejecting is non-conceptual). But it is the last one that is ever made: henceforward, there will only be acts of the will, and even decisions to be creative will be determined only by one's current ideas. This entails that conceptual thought is to henceforth be my highest priority, and intuition merely its tool. For, if I could transcend all conceptual thought by intuition, it follows that in my actions I could transcend my conflicting priorities also, for these are all articulated in thought. However, if this is not the case, then the dire result of my universal decision to choose will over transcendence is that spiritual freedom is now subjugated to the mental bondage of thoughts and concepts, and darkness descends, severing contact with my higher self (see Chapter 1). Now, I no longer know who I am, nor where I am going.

In order to escape from the interminable treadmill of thought, such lost souls, acting only from will, now need an experience of enlightenment or redemption to rescue them. These are those unfortunates considered throughout this book who, having fallen prey to alienation by their adverse experience of life, are now imprisoned by choices determined purely by their own existing concepts and nothing else. Consequently they languish in limbo, trapped from experiencing real freedom.

Why do we need Enlightenment?

Being born with the ability to form concepts, it is not implausible to suggest that we are therefore born with the capacity for mystical experience since, as I have argued, these experiences constitute our insight into new concepts before we have them, as well as providing such innate capacities as humour. Above all, they enable us to transcend the dilemmas we encounter in life, so as to judge a middle way. Taken together, these mystical capacities make us human, and we might surely expect the nature of what makes us most human to be innate. Indeed, when we lose ourselves in the fathomless eyes of a newborn baby, it is not difficult to believe that in this innateness we are nevertheless encountering the wisdom of the ages. Hence, if we were to somehow lose this instinctive recognition, this capacity for mystical experience, it is unlikely to be due to philosophical scepticism alone, since such recognition is profound and independent of any prevailing doctrines or theories. Yet many adults have forgotten the mystical nature with which they were born, and stand in need of enlightenment. How is this possible?

Rather than by doctrines and theories, a loss of spiritual insight is more likely to be emotional in origin, such as by physical or mental shock. For example, if one person A has power over another person B, then the options open to B can become severely restricted by his fear of A. Thus, the will of B becomes the will of A, and the transcendence of this will by B becomes curtailed by his fear of A. For, each time B transcends the concepts in their shared language he may be met with punishment and scorn, and so new meanings, the key to his humanity, cannot be created by him. As a result B may begin to feel dehumanized.

Consider, for instance, a daughter with an overbearing father whose love she craves, but who has unrelentingly high standards. As a result, she feels she can only please him by performing well: winning a medal at dancing, high exam grades and the like, with the ever-present fear of failure. Indicating her to a visitor, her father smiles at her and says casually, 'I'm sure she won't disappoint me.' This habitual way of subtly ratcheting up the pressure, under the guise of seeming not to care, acts as a form of emotional blackmail that fills her with dread.

Similarly, Andre Agassi (see Chapter 1) describes how, as a seven year old boy, his father in a more direct manner tried to turn him into a tennis-playing automaton:

I know there are few children in the world who could have seen that ball, let alone hit it. But I take no pride in my reflexes, and get no credit. It's what I'm supposed to do. Every hit is expected, every miss a crisis.

My father says that if I hit 2,500 balls each day, I'll hit 17,500 balls each week, and at the end of one year I'll have hit nearly one million balls. He believes in math. Numbers, he says, don't lie. A child who hits one million balls each year will be unbeatable.

Andre Agassi, *Open*

Finally, consider the quite different situation of a helicopter pilot in war-torn Vietnam, appalled at the horrors he has been indirectly ordered to inflict upon innocent villagers.

In all these cases the subject is forced into acts foreign to their nature which dehumanizes them; each in its way is surely an example of traumatic stress, either physical or emotional. In each case their actions are under the control of another: the two children were controlled by fear of their fathers, the pilot is controlled by military discipline. In each scenario, transcendence of the will becomes impossible, instead making each agent into a tool or puppet of another person's will.

We thus see how transcendence, instead of reigning supreme in accordance with our inborn nature, can in particular scenarios or relationships be forced into being subjugated to the rigid concepts employed by the will of another person, or delegated to impersonal rules. In this way, the innate source of our sense of worth is being dismissed or ignored, affronting our self-esteem. But worse may be to follow. For the physical or mental punishment at failing to please authority may produce a pain so intense that it causes you to deny your own inner nature entirely: you betray your own soul. This is often the real context in which the wrong existential choice is actually made: we now see that it is not a merely intellectual decision, but may be fraught with emotion; one's life is held in the balance.

For, in such a case you may learn to repress your higher nature, not just in those particular situations which penalized it, but *in all situations whatsoever*. In the above example, one consequence might be that the daughter not only loses her love for her father, she loses her capacity to love anyone at all. It is almost as if she flips over into a different mental state in which she becomes cold and impersonal and appears to lack any feelings about anything. For, only by making oneself numb, dissociating oneself from one's feelings, can one carry out orders foreign to one's inmost being. This can lead, in the extreme case, to making oneself into a mere puppet, an instrument of an alien will. By doing this, the daughter protects herself from the intense suffering she feels at the rejection, by her father, of her inner self. For, to cope with her father's rejection, she now finds that *she has herself to reject her own being*, in order to anticipate her father's will. The resulting mental state of numbness we call *depression*, since it masks an acute anguish, due to fixed thoughts and concepts 'pressing down' on her. The onlooker is now greeted by dull and lifeless eyes, and a hard shell of indifference or apathy.

This is the one particular kind of depression upon which I wish to focus: what we might call alienation or existential despair. Of course there are other kinds of depression (e.g. anorexia) manifesting a fixation on only one area of life (e.g. physical appearance). However, this is the one, despite its origin possibly only being the traumatic stress in one specific situation, which we may nevertheless associate with the *rejection of life itself*. This is because the faculty it corrodes or disables, our transcendence of concepts in general, was not merely specific to that one traumatic situation, but affects the subject's response to *all* situations in life, since there are no situations in which concepts are not used. From the evidence, such depression appears to originate with a psychological submission to the rigid and inflexible imposition of one particular set of concepts, which then becomes generalized to *all possible concepts*.[1] As a result, far from giving precedence to transcendence, instead transcendence has been abolished altogether, to be replaced by a straitjacket of concepts implanted either externally or internally. And in the absence of transcendence one is no longer aware of any higher self; instead of living, one is now merely existing, sleepwalking through life.

The final consequence of this reaction is therefore a universal repression of all of one's natural impulses of transcendence by means of the unremitting gloom of alienation. It is the experience I identified initially (Chapter 1) as a *loss of identity*, of no longer comprehending who you are, or how to live, so movingly expressed both by Tolstoy and by Andre Agassi, as well as by Sylvia Plath. It is a new psychological state which we can distinguish not only from enlightenment, but from normal living and loving, and is familiarly called 'losing your soul'. It conveys the plight of Beckett's *Unnameable* (Chapter 4) in trying but failing to find the real silence, and it is the state common not only to all Sartre's cases of 'bad faith' but also to his 'authenticity' acknowledging the human condition. For, I have argued that it is not really the human condition at all, but is a pathological state.

What is interesting about this pathology is how an intense experience in just one area of life can have such a generalized effect on one's approach to life as a whole. My thesis is that a trauma can come to affect, not just our particular human relationships, but our capacity *to transcend thought in general*, i.e. our very concept of reality. The girl's relationship with her father destroys her confidence in every area of life, the helicopter pilot's depression affects every choice he makes. Somehow, one period of traumatic stress, if it dominates one's life for that period, can affect all of one's subsequent *cognitive* development. The habit of repressing her spiritual freedom in the presence of her father seemed, at a certain point, to have switched the daughter into a different psychological state. In this new state, her spiritual freedom was gone permanently – not just with respect to her father – but in all areas of life, present and future. This is how Freud famously explained the prevailing lack of sexual freedom, but it may also be true that our lack of spiritual freedom may be equally due to childhood conditioning. However, where Freud might say that the greatest grief suffered by the daughter is her rejection by her father, we are here saying it is the loss of her soul. For there always was something she loved more than her father, namely: her intuition, her very being, her capacity to love at all. It is her own rejection of all of these that is surely her greatest grief.

Shutting down one's transcendence can make it incomprehensibly difficult to get it back; temporarily hiding one's self may make it impossibly hard to find it again, and in this way the loss may become permanent. Above all, abolishing our higher self may abolish the functions that the higher self performed: not only as to self-esteem and the capacity to love, but also the ability to adjust to new situations, resolve conflicts and form new concepts. In other words, we lose a *significant region of human intelligence*. We are still able to think and calculate, but we are unable to create new meaning, since life itself has no meaning. We no longer have the ability to transcend our will, nor to understand anything in the absence of thought, as we no longer know what these mean; we have entered into the dark night of the soul.

Although the cases of the daughter and the helicopter pilot were very different, they nevertheless seem to be united by the structure of their depression, if not its cause. For in each case, actions are now determined only by control and calculation, and not by transcendence because, whatever the chain of events that brought it about, transcendence *is no longer permitted*. This, unbeknownst to them, is, I believe, the real source of their private grief. All of this is what is implied by losing your soul. To be alienated is therefore to be, in certain respects, dysfunctional; it is, as Tolstoy said, as if 'something had broken within me on which my life had always rested' (Chapter 1). If it does not terminate in suicide, this pattern of depression can become a lifelong handicap.

It has been the argument of this work that, once having lost one's soul, having fallen from grace, the only way to restore it is by an equally dramatic act of redemption, of being 'born again', in which the will that originally seized power is once more surrendered, enabling the psychological state to switch back to its original state before it was corrupted. This we call 'enlightenment'. If the daughter fails to regain her former self by attaining enlightenment, then upon becoming a mother, the iron control she imposes on herself is now liable to be inflicted in turn upon her own children. In this way, spiritual repression filters down the generations like a hereditary illness.

But let us inquire further into the initial step: by what mechanism, if it is indeed the case, can an emotional experience concerning just one set of concepts during childhood, one particular relationship or relationships, then go on to affect our use of *all* our other concepts, present and future? In reply, I should like to suggest a possibly unexpected link with the satori experience of Zen. For, just as universal enlightenment may in Zen have been produced by a single sudden experience, so its converse, the universal loss of transcendence, may, as we have seen, also be produced by a single kind of experience, possibly a traumatic one. The joy of a singular experience of transcending the will can conversely be mirrored by the anguish of a singular experience of subjugating that joy to the will. Where one experience awoke us to the possibility of new meaning, the other experience deadens that prospect, confining us hereafter only to the prison of those meanings we already have. Each of these salutary experiences reflects one of the poles of the existential choice.

Now, the existential choice is not purely conceptual, and so our negative decision to subjugate ourself to concepts cannot be conceptual either, even though conceptual choices are all we will thereafter permit ourself. What form therefore can such a decision take? Surely, as with the positive choice of transcendence, a singular negative experience can be used as an *exemplar* for all future experiences. As before, we take note of the sharp experiential contrast between transcendence and thought; only here, instead of choosing transcendence, we choose thought.

Doubtless we have our motives, to avoid the pain of our oppressor, but the step was a fatal one: we have lost our soul. And now my question is that, just as in Zen one singular choice of transcendence may act as an exemplar or fulcrum for all such choices in the future, so conversely is it not possible, when presented with a particular painful choice, that one singular decision to currently eliminate transcendence may equally act as an exemplar for all such decisions in the future? In the examples given, conceptual thought (repression) was, ex hypothesi, being chosen, not out of preference, but to avoid the pain of being punished (by a parent or teacher, or a military court martial) for choosing transcendence, i.e. for following your heart.

If this traumatic decision is comprehended as an exemplar then, in making this choice, we have (non-conceptually) resolved that for all the dilemmas we meet in life in the future we will always put will and calculation first, crushing or repressing the spiritual self and denying ourself fulfilment. It is certainly a depressing prospect. The thesis is that it is possible to make this decision about conceptual thought without itself using conceptual thought; and that, just like its mirror-image satori, perhaps it can all be implicated in a single negative experience of rejecting the very transcendence that satori embraces.

This then is my explanation of alienation from life: that, far from being a recognition of the Human Condition, it is on the contrary a pathological state – yet without being an illness. It is often in practice preceded by traumatic experience of some kind, which can then prove pivotal in a person's life by being treated by them, fatefully, as an experiential exemplar symbolizing the whole of reality. The temporary rejection, for one's own protection, of transcendence in a currently stressful situation can disastrously prompt a generalized rejection of transcendence for all future situations in favour of the exclusive use only of thought and will. This is a life from which all personal fulfilment has been purged by the loss of identity produced by a form of mental bondage.

What is rational?

However, in the absence of any trauma, rational thought may seem harmless enough; for it is just the pursuit and application of knowledge by privately framing and testing hypotheses with no inducement to eliminate any personal understanding obtained by transcendence. There is no reason, therefore, why the two mental processes cannot coexist within the same person; in Christian terms, Will can be compatible with Grace. However, the Cartesian belief that Will provides the only kind of knowledge, the refusal to accept any knowledge other than clear and distinct ideas, does supply an intellectual basis for rejecting transcendence as self-knowledge. Intellectually, such scepticism lays the foundation for our modern conception of rationality, and says that, in order to be meaningful, the tramp in the cartoon must only be offered factual thoughts in answer to his question, and nothing more.

It seems, though, that there is no logical reason why the tramp should not adhere to the hypothetico-deductive method (or ask the clerk) with regard only to factual information, but nevertheless transcend all these thoughts with regard to self-knowledge and judging practical courses of action. In other words, there is no logical requirement for the tramp to make the Cartesian assumption. Scientific method need not in itself imply scepticism about other kinds of knowledge. For to make the Cartesian assumption about one's own life, by denying self-knowledge because it does not comprise factual information (clear and distinct ideas), may be to commit a disastrous personal error. However, the error may not necessarily have the effects it had, for example, on Tolstoy, for it may only be an intellectual error, with no emotional commitment to it. Philosophical beliefs need not have the same impact as traumatic stress.

For, real life is not often purely about the disinterested

pursuit of such knowledge, but about making practical decisions. In many situations the most practical course is indeed not to attempt to reconceptualize a contradiction, but quite simply to choose which of the conflicting statements is the right one; we cannot have them both. E.g. reconciling conflicting totals in a financial balance sheet, or avoiding booking two halls for the same concert. In practical life contradictions usually spell failure or error and cannot be permitted; in order to think productively in a disciplined environment, it is normally necessary to reject logical inconsistency. It is only in big or personal decisions – e.g. unique moral or political dilemmas, or questions of judgement or design – where it may become imperative to think of a new idea. Here we can permit ourselves the luxury of transcending apparent contradictions. However, contradicting oneself is seldom very helpful in routine situations, including the rule-governed working environments in which most people are professionally employed.

Often though, we may think our situation is more restricted than it really is. In professional situations it may not be possible to alter the terms of reference; but in Sartre's more personal example of divided loyalty, we saw it might be quite beneficial to do so. Why then did the son nevertheless not transcend his conflicting loyalties to find a middle way? We may say perhaps that it was because people now mostly equate rationality only with logical deduction and induction from whatever they can conceive, employing only the concepts they already possess, and endeavouring at all costs to avoid contradictions. They then perhaps allow this stereotyped (Cartesian) view of rationality to curtail their intuition of new concepts. On this view, the embracing of contradictions must seem the very height of irrationality. So perhaps we may conclude that the son was simply doing nothing more than manifesting his own conception of rational thought, which forbade him to transcend his contra-diction, believing instead that logic required him to choose one given option or the other.

If it is Aristotelian logic that forces us in life to choose between the two tigers, then it is the Cartesian view of knowledge that prevents us seeing the strawberry, precluding the possibility of a middle way. Together these make up our modern view of rational behaviour. Thus, apart from traumatic stress, we now see that there is also a much more prosaic explanation of unenlightened behaviour: it may simply be held to be rational. Conversely, enlightened behaviour may be seen as irrational. For enlightenment alters our very conception of rationality; it alters how we use our own mind. One consequence of this is that, by educating our children to be rational in the modern sense, we may be said to be training them to be unenlightened.

It is by assuming modern-day rationality that one may in practice fail to transcend contradictions; i.e. by assuming with Descartes that clear thoughts which avoid contradictions are the only knowledge. In this way we see only the options presented, and are blind to what is intimated by intuition beyond the limits of thought. We proceed, due to caution or method, only along the preconceived corridors of thought. This then reinforces our continuing confinement by current concepts, to the detriment of innovation. It is in this way that a tedious life can superficially resemble an anguished one, whilst in reality being generated only by rules and academic standards, rather than by any traumatic stress in the past. Here, the existential choice might be said to be imposed more mildly by intellectual conviction or educational conformity, rather than emotionally. It surely begins to appear that we should recognize that enlightenment provides us, by contrast, with new and improved ways of being rational.

The two competing views of rationality yield two views of the human condition of how we understand human beings to engage with the world. They are the two extremes of mystic joy on the one hand, and existential despair on the other. These extremes are related, in particular, via the manner of their mutual inter-conversion: by the fact that one of them is precisely the rejection of what the other embraces. What they both have in common is that neither of them is empirical, i.e. each is to some extent impervious to circumstances, since both express our attitude to life as a whole, regardless of circumstances. It is surely for this reason that, just as no good fortune can ever cheer the existential cynic, so equally no misfortune can depress the enlightened mystic. It is because what they both have in common is a conviction that social and material circumstances are not the most important things in life, but that life as a whole is what matters.

It is this outlook which religion also traditionally espouses. For example religions normally value asceticism, and extoll the virtues of self-sacrifice, at the same time criticizing our nearsighted preoccupation with material things. And the great life-changing transformation of enlightenment, converting us from one view of our human condition into another is, in one form or another, that with which all the major religions have been concerned. In my proposed rationalization of this process, I have borrowed religious terminology such as soul, will, spiritual freedom and enlightenment itself. In the final part of my narrative I now want to make this comparison with religious beliefs more explicit.

We can, for instance, now employ the terms 'heaven' and 'hell' as psychological terms describing states of mind in this life, instead of places we go after death. On this basis 'heaven' would describe enlightenment, and 'hell' describes existential despair. Moreover, I believe that in some sense this too must be the real meaning of these terms in Christianity. For the Christian heaven must surely be guaranteed to bring joy to its occupants – but how can any mere place or set of circumstances be infallibly guaranteed to achieve this? If a depressive were to visit such a paradise she could still turn it to ashes in her mind, since this is the nature of depression: there are no circumstances, however wondrous, that can cheer it, for the very *capacity for wonder has been lost.*

By the same token, the depressive is already in hell, since it is the worst suffering a human mind can experience, so there is no mere *place* that can inflict it; it is something we do to ourself. Conversely of course, a religious visionary such as the Buddha may be said to be in heaven already, he sees heaven in the lilies of the field that toil not, in the birds of the air, in the pattering raindrops. There is nowhere he can go, no paradise which can improve upon it. So the external vocabulary used by religions must, to the extent that it is true, be capable of being reinterpreted internally, i.e. in terms of psychological states and dispositions.

Between the extremes of heaven and hell lies the limbo in which most of us contrive to live. This is the normal life lived mainly for the sake of human relationships: moral and social reputation, professional recognition, personal love and family affection. Nor must we leave out of the reckoning the idealism often inspired by social standards: the principles for which we fight, the religious and political causes we believe in. In this kind of life, genuinely spiritual feelings, whether positive or negative, play a relatively minor role, if they figure at all. This is not to say there is no transcendence of concepts used in directing normal living: on the contrary, intuition is frequently employed in the pursuit of all these lesser goals and principles – and even in doing wrong. But in each case, intuition is only being used as a tool in the service of some desired principle or relationship, seldom as an *end in itself.* A life of spiritual fulfilment, however, requires not only this, but indeed requires transcendence to be the supreme end, by which all other ends are measured.

Adam and Eve

Given that enlightenment, and hence the Existential Choice, cannot be put into words, the great religions have used allegories and parables to try to symbolize the universal predicament of man. One such myth in Judaism, Christianity and Islam is the origin of mankind according to the story of Adam and Eve. I propose here to demonstrate how the Fall of man and Original Sin can be interpreted, not as in the Bible via the actions of typical humans, but in abstract rational terms, via dimensions of the universal mind of man, and the nature of human cognition.

The essence of the story is that Adam, the first man, was created in the image of God in a state of childlike innocence, living in a paradise called Eden, but then was tempted to eat fruit forbidden him by God from the tree of knowledge of good and evil. Thereupon, he and Eve, and all their descendants, were banished from paradise forever more. It is a powerful tale, simply told, full of resonances: psychological, ethical and sexual. It will be my aim to interpret each of the elements in this tale as broad psychological states and attributes having universal relevance not just to morality, but to knowledge and reason.

Initially, Adam, because of his innocence, is presented as incapable of choosing between good and evil because he does not know the difference. This is a moral interpretation, but it seems there is a cognitive consideration also since, consistent with his innocence, God thereby allowed man to bestow names upon all the animals:

And the man gave names to all cattle, and to the fowl of heaven, to every beast of the field...

Thus, this moral innocence also appears to be associated with our ability to form concepts. In simply being able to *recognize* when something is or is not a cow, Adam, at this stage, is granted only the power of forming concepts but not apparently the power of thought; that will only come later. By 'Adam' I understand the Mind, and it seems now that the mind is capable only of forming concepts, but not yet capable of the more sophisticated task of

combining them together into truths or falsehoods. At this stage
Adam is not able to say of what he recognizes as a cow, that it is
not a cow. In other words, he can only utter truths, not falsehoods; he can only give voice to his simple recognition, much
like the innocence of a baby learning its first words. He is not yet
capable of thought or language, since thoughts and sentences are
capable of being used to say what is false as well as what is true.
I believe this latter capacity resides in the fruit of the tree of
knowledge of good and evil, which God forbids man to eat.

In the Bible, the serpent persuades Eve to eat fruit from the
tree of knowledge:

[1]Now the serpent was more subtle than any beast of the field which
the Lord God had made. And he said unto the woman, Yea, hath God
said, Ye shall not eat of every tree of the garden? [2]And the woman
said unto the serpent, We may eat of the fruit of the trees of the
garden: [3]But of the fruit of the tree which *is* in the midst of the
garden, God hath said, Ye shall not eat of it, neither shall ye touch it,
lest ye die. [4]And the serpent said unto the woman, Ye shall not surely
die: [5]For God doth know that in the day ye eat thereof, then your
eyes shall be opened, and ye shall be as gods, knowing good and
evil. [6]And when the woman saw that the tree *was* good for food, and
that it *was* pleasant to the eyes, and a tree to be desired to make *one*
wise, she took of the fruit thereof, and did eat, and gave also unto
her husband with her; and he did eat. [7]And the eyes of them both
were opened, and they knew that they *were* naked; and they sewed
fig leaves together, and made themselves aprons.

First let us dispose of what may appear a methodological difficulty, for it does seem that these conversations do employ
language and thought already, and so how can the latter only be
a consequence of partaking of the fruit? However, on my interpretation, the instructions of God are not really linguistic or
conceptual at all, but rather the non-conceptual or pre-linguistic

promptings of transcendence; this surely is how the biblical God is to be understood in his communication with man. Similarly, the words of the serpent may be meant to signify other pre-linguistic movements of the mind, as well as the subsequent serpentine processes of verbal thought. On a cognitive interpretation, the fruit now stands for items of knowledge, perhaps available to sense perception; the hierarchical structure of knowledge may be evoked by a tree between whose forks the serpent may weave his way, just as we weave our way between alternative thoughts by logical reasoning.

The serpent offers the fruit to Eve, and thereby to Adam; this is the Temptation, and the consequence of the resulting Sin was that 'the eyes of both of them were opened'. What exactly does this mean? It means that before eating the fruit they had been, in a certain sense, blind. But blind to what? Blind to a vital prerequisite for thought and language: the possibility of falsehood, of thoughts being untrue as well as true. Without this possibility, thoughts that are supposedly 'true' fail to distinguish when a state of affairs obtains from when it does not obtain. If a cow were 'truly' said to be grazing, *regardless* of whether it actually is grazing, then the utterance fails to distinguish whether it is grazing or not. Without falsehood, truth is of no value. However, once Adam has the full capacity for thought and language, then any concept can in principle be ascribed to any object, with the resulting thought being sometimes true, sometimes false. A false thought is as much a thought as a true thought, and while only the latter is called knowledge, we need to understand both, in order to grasp the underlying nature of knowledge. Viewed thus, knowledge of the tree of good and evil provides knowledge of true and false as a special case of good and evil, for along with the capacity of words to be false comes the human capacity to deliberately use them falsely. Thus, words facilitate deception and insincerity, and (other things being equal) sincerity is good, and insincerity is 'evil'.

And so our thoughts and speech are being likened to moral choices, since they often decide whether a concept is to be paired falsely or truly with an object. With the advent of thought and speech, man's eyes are opened to the possibilities of such false pairings: we may say Adam and Eve have now lost their *pre-logical innocence*; it seems that only by being innocent of true and false could they spontaneously be themselves. For it is only with the deliberate use of the will that thought and speech become possible.

As well as the cognitive interpretation there is also the more familiar sexual interpretation, whereby Adam and Eve were blind to their sexuality; and then their eyes were opened to their being male and female. This was surely how their 'nakedness' differed from mere nudity: the realization after The Fall that Adam was male and Eve was female. In this way they could 'know' each other sexually. By subsequently hiding their bodies with 'aprons', they could pretend to lack this knowledge; nakedness would then mean dropping this pretence, i.e. admitting to their knowledge of male and female; but pure nudity, lacking this knowledge, is no longer possible. Thus, as well as their pre-logical innocence, they have also lost their sexual innocence, since only by being embarrassed at their knowledge of each other do they now feel naked. In this way, clothing seems to resemble language in providing the prospect of concealing or denying what you know.

When Eve offered Adam the fruit,[2] so thought itself became seductive to them, for now that they see how concepts can be peeled off an object, the way clothes can be peeled off a person, they are not able to unlearn this knowledge, either about words or about clothes: i.e. that both can be used to conceal. And it is not only thoughts that are attractive, but the very mechanism (Logic) of thought itself seems to become seductive, perhaps because of the pleasures it brings under human control. Because it brings pleasures of the senses, thought itself becomes pleasurable, and causes us to want it.

The Church refers to this as the sin of Pride, because Adam (I use 'Adam' to henceforward embrace Eve) ignored God's express instruction not to eat fruit from the tree of knowledge, saying it will make him die. However, Adam does eat the fruit, and yet does not die; does this in turn make God a liar? No – I believe what was meant was not physical but spiritual death, the death of something in his mind essential to a meaningful life; in other words: the forbidden fruit brings the loss of his soul, a living death. How does it do this? By making the effects of this momentary existential choice be everlasting, so that Adam and Eve can never regain their innocence. The reason they are expelled permanently from paradise seems to be that once we have attained to thought and language, it inevitably appears to us to now be the *only* path to truth, and we forget the other path of innocence and our non-conceptual sense of self. The new premeditated criterion of truth seems to completely eclipse the old spontaneous one. But why should this be; why should our realization (as Descartes articulated) that falsehood is an ever-present risk cancel any other kind of non-factual knowledge, such as our sense of self, that appears to neglect this possibility?

It seems, adapting Kuhn, to be a paradigm-shift in Adam's very concept of truth; once he has seen how any concept can be false of an object, he can never forget this fact. Like any conceptual revolution (such as the Greek invention of democracy, or Pasteur's discovery of bacteria), we can never go back to what we may call our preconceptual innocence. For, once our 'eyes are opened' to a new concept, we cannot forget what we have seen; and this may even be true of the very concept of truth itself. For now, by comparison, Adam's earlier expressions of simple recognition may come to him to seem primitive or naïve, and thereafter he is naturally tempted into making the Cartesian assumption that what is actually *meant* by knowledge can never be anything other than factual thoughts which are true or false (see Fig. 1).

This compulsion is, I believe, the underlying cognitive meaning of the Temptation and Fall of Adam, for deception and insincerity have now become permanent options for him, from which he cannot extricate himself. We may indeed also equate this with what Sartre called: the burden of freedom.

More particularly, within any human mind the response to the tree of knowledge can now be seen as symbolizing the Existential Choice; in other words, the decision as to how to live your life. Viewed thus, the dialogues with God and with the serpent symbolize the heroic struggle in the mind between the vastly differing impulses of the will on the one hand, and its transcendence on the other; for the choice is between which of them shall ultimately govern my life. Accordingly, by God's punishment of Adam, we mean therefore the consequences inflicted upon the human mind by its own rejection of transcendence, for the latter is exactly what is meant by 'disobeying God'. The Bible presents some of these consequences in the following words:

> [17]And unto Adam he said, Because thou hast hearkened unto the voice of thy wife, and hast eaten of the tree, of which I commanded thee, saying, Thou shalt not eat of it: cursed *is* the ground for thy sake; in sorrow shalt thou eat *of* it all the days of thy life; [18]Thorns also and thistles shall it bring forth to thee; and thou shalt eat the herb of the field; [19]In the sweat of thy face shalt thou eat bread, till thou return unto the ground; for out of it wast thou taken: for dust thou *art*, and unto dust shalt thou return.

Adam is expelled from paradise (no longer permitted to experience ecstasy), and is condemned to a lifetime of toil ('in the sweat of thy face, shalt thou eat bread'). This is because, having tasted the fruits of thought, he now (just like Beckett's *Unnameable*, Chapter 4) cannot rid himself of thoughts. This means he cannot forget the permanent possibility of falsehood, as well as of truth, with its attendant consequences of doubt and insecurity; for the only kind of knowledge now available to him is the knowledge of facts whereby, for any given object, concepts can be either true of that object, or false of it. He must now use this knowledge into which he has so foolishly plunged himself in order to extract sustenance, 'bread', from nature. By the disciplined work (the sweat of his face) of constantly adjusting his actions according to what is true and what is false, that knowledge and logical reasoning which he was so desirous of tasting shall now be his lot 'all the days of thy life'.

By contrast, we saw that both Tolstoy's Levin and the Zen swordsman (Chapter 2) were able to be physically successful, despite abdicating from thought, i.e. by somehow restoring their innocence. Recall that when the Zen master played the stroke, he had no doubts because he employed no concepts, whereas his pupil, by contrast, was thinking thoughts p, q... about each move, causing him to fail. For as soon as we think a thought p, we immediately introduce the possibility of not-p, but the master, lacking any conceptual intent p, entertains no such conception of not-p and is consequently fearless, having in his head no conception of failure. It is as if the Zen master experiences the same innocence Adam possessed before partaking of conceptual knowledge.

But now that Adam has embarked upon a life of thought and calculation, the Bible seems to be telling us that the blissful option, free of thought, is no longer available to Adam and his descendants, since it seems to require a return to an innocence he has lost forever. Nevertheless, it is the doctrine of religions (including Christianity) that this state is not, as suggested in Genesis, irreversible, and that salvation is at hand. For, although we cannot ever regain that state of innocence we had before we had any thoughts at all, it has been evinced here that it might nevertheless be possible to attain a mystical state transcending whatever conceptual thoughts we currently do have. Christianity requires this to be attained via Christ, but I have argued rationally on behalf of a cognitive version of Buddhist enlightenment.

It should be abundantly clear that the complete absence of thought in a newborn baby (and Adam before the Fall) is not at all a desirable state for us, for we do need thoughts in order to make our way in life. Nevertheless, something of the same peace of mind associated with such innocence is, I have suggested, available to adult human beings. While we continue to participate in disciplined work and rational thought, still we can acquaint ourselves with the limits of such thought and, as we have seen, this acquaintance can never be established purely by thought itself. With endless thought alone, we are on a kind of treadmill, and are indeed, as a result, excluded from paradise.

But now I am arguing that a form of redemption is possible, whereby man can be rescued from the Fall. For, as well as being familiar with thought, it is possible at the same time, via a meditative grasp of its contradictions, to discern its limits, and by means of ambiguity to transcend those limits. And, whereas the original innocence in the Garden may have been naïve, this new innocence is sophisticated, since it now has full knowledge of thought, but prefers to choose transcendence. This ambiguous sophistication is surely the inscrutability we have always associated with the wisdom of the East. For now, unlike Adam, when we think a sentence is true we are not necessarily committed to thinking its negation is false for we allow that, under reinterpretation, its negation may also be true.

Adam's Fall was due to his knowledge of falsehood. However, we have now introduced a new factor into the story: the feasibility of contradiction; in this way we can slay the serpent, permitting the possibility of redemption and a return to paradise. For Adam's loss of innocence was due to his embracing of knowledge and free will, both of which require conceptual thought, the ascription of concepts to objects. By contrast contradictions, while composed of concepts, never do express conceptual thoughts. Hence the embracing of contradictions as such is never the desire for particular knowledge, nor the pursuit of any objective.

Before the Fall, contradictions were, of course, not possible for Adam, because only thoughts can contradict and, thought had, as we might say, *not been invented yet*. And then, even after the Fall, they signified only confusion or conflict in our thinking. It is only with our modern sophistication that we can comprehend not only the contradicting thoughts themselves, but comprehend how to go beyond the Logic of thought by creating ambiguity, enabling them to provide entirely new meaning. So the form which this comprehending takes does of course then not, as St Teresa discovered (Chapter 3), consist of thoughts themselves, but of a special experience (union with God) of transcending thought, an experience forfeited by Adam.

By comprehending contradictions, we are then enabled to anticipate the truth of future thoughts that we cannot yet think. We do this by somehow recognizing instances of a future concept as they arise, without clearly conceiving what a false instance would be like. Consequently, like Adam before the Fall, man is now in a sense able once more to grasp truths *without grasping the possibility of their falsehood*. In this way, innocence may be said to be restored to mankind and we are redeemed. From a cognitive standpoint, notice that the basis of both innocence and redemption is similar, for our enlightened grasp of certain contradictions anticipates new concepts, and also Adam was giving names to the animals; hence both redemption and innocence are expressions of concept formation.

Marlowe's *Dr Faustus*

Adam, on my account, contrary to the Church, was not guilty of pride, since he had no inflated idea of himself; nor was his error due to mistrust, desire, doubt or insecurity, all of which afflict modern man. In fact, his actions were not the result of any negative emotion whatsoever, only the pleasure of intellectual curiosity, and perhaps forgetfulness of his instructions. So we may wonder: wasn't his punishment a little severe? Other works of art and literature have indirectly addressed the seemingly disproportionate consequences of making the wrong existential choice, and I shall discuss two of them here, namely Marlowe's *Dr Faustus*, and *The Trial*, a novel by Franz Kafka.

In Marlowe's play, Faustus does indeed suffer from the sin of pride, as he desires fame, power and riches, as well as knowledge for its own sake; he finds that the inner rewards of having already done good are inadequate for him. In fact he is in general unimpressed by what the soul has to offer and dismisses philosophy, medicine and theology as not concrete enough and not providing enough power over events. Like Adam he has a pure thirst for knowledge and is inquisitive about the planets and the universe, like a modern scientist. He resorts to necromancy, summoning up the forces of darkness, and is rewarded by the arrival of Mephistopheles, an agent of Lucifer, who offers him anything in the world for twenty-four years, but there is just one drawback: he must surrender his soul to Lucifer at the end of that time. Faustus willingly agrees and fatefully signs a contract written in his own blood:

> I cut mine arm and with my proper blood
> Assure my soul to be great Lucifer's,
> Chief lord and regent of perpetual night.

What is interesting is that Faustus at this time appears to have no difficulty transacting this bargain, even though Mephistopheles, upon inquiry, gives him a clear warning of what is entailed:

> Why this is hell, nor am I out of it.
> Think'st thou that I, who saw the face of God,
> And tasted the eternal joys of heaven,

Am not tormented with ten thousand hells
In being deprived of everlasting bliss?
O Faustus, leave these frivolous demands,
Which strike terror to my fainting soul.

But Faustus seems not to comprehend what will be lost, and simply replies:

What, is great Mephistopheles so passionate
For being deprived of the joys of heaven?
Learn thou of Faustus manly fortitude,
And scorn those joys thou never shalt possess.

In his bravado he seems to regard the joys of heaven merely as being comparable to worldly pleasures, having little conception of their real magnitude or significance in making worldly pleasures possible at all. By the same token we can perhaps infer that he has no real conception of the value of his soul, or its significance – which is the reason he feels able to part with it so cheerfully. Later he remarks, commenting on Mephistopheles' information that hell can be here and now, 'How now in hell? I'll willingly be damned here! What, walking, disputing etc...' His bravura seems to be because he mistakenly judges all the potential future experiences of his life, not as a whole, but only by their individual conceptual content.

In many ways the desires of Faustus have been met by modern science and technology, such as travelling through the air to distant places, witnessing moving images of persons long dead, eating fresh fruit from foreign countries. Indeed, the manipulations of symbols in the incantations of Faustus: 'characters and erring stars, by which the spirits are enforced to rise' superficially resemble the calculations of applied mathematics, invoking the mechanical laws of nature. Faustus has entrusted his entire future to a methodology, just as we may say the scientist, and by association the rest of us, entrusts his projects to experiment and calculation, the hypothetico-deductive method. It may be possible, at some level, to trace the seeds of our modern world of cynicism, environmental decay and genocide ultimately to the alienating aspects of the scientific (and Cartesian) method, viewing this as a Faustian pact in which the human race, while it has gained untold riches, may nevertheless be said to have sold its soul.

It may equally seem that this is a disproportionate price to pay for scientific knowledge; after all, most individual scientists are apparently innocent and well-intentioned. In the particular case of Faustus, Marlowe never explains why the forfeiture of his soul is an appropriate price for him to pay for controlling nature. In particular, he is not arguing that Faustus deserves his fate because he gets corrupted by his power, since it was the price agreed from the outset. Nor was it power that made him proud, for he was proud from the start. Further, the price could not even be justified as appropriate by anticipating that Faustus *must* in any case become corrupted, as a result of his power, for this quite simply never happened. Rather, like Adam, Faustus mainly displayed a pure desire for knowledge and when he acquires knowledge and power he does not use it to perform evil or even harm anybody. Instead, he behaves in a way which is apparently innocent: he performs childish pranks on the pope, performs stunts to astound the nobility, and indulges his sexual desires with Helen of Troy.

So, without being evil, Faustus is nevertheless consigned to hell. Why is this? It is because the tale is not really intended to depict the chronological history of a particular man, but is a parable of the priorities in life, an allegory symbolizing the existential choice, the struggle between will and grace inside each of us. And the price of making the wrong choice is, as Mephistopheles says, to be living in hell in the here and now. As in the case of Adam, the cognitive rationale is that if *in every action in life* I adhere to impersonal methods and principles (such as logic or science), which I always place before faith or grace, then I am making the wrong existential choice and thereby placing my soul in jeopardy. The structure of *Dr Faustus* as a whole symbolizes such a commitment, regardless of the personal goodwill or ill will to which he puts these methods. It is not whether his will is good or bad that is his sin, but the fact that Faustus has made the fateful decision for his will to be the overriding factor in determining his choices in life. This commitment is what is meant by signing his contract with Lucifer. Correspondingly, Faustus believes that the pious attainments of faith are tame and illusory, since only concrete results are of any consequence. In cognitive terms, this surely means that in his head Faustus has decided, like a modern existentialist, to cling to conceptual thought and self-consciousness, thereby denying himself the possibility of acting from intuitions and self-awareness. Instead this means operating purely by will, and however well-intentioned that will may be, in the absence of any grace transcending it the consequences for one's life are quite literally unimaginable.

The Trial by Franz Kafka

In the case of Kafka, the Fall of man is depicted more subtly for, by contrast, in *The Trial* Joseph K is presented as meek and has no inflated ideas about himself and only ever wants to do the right thing. In Kafka's novel the innocence or guilt of Adam is symbolized by legal innocence or guilt, with the mind of man being judged by a court of law. In *The Trial* K is arrested and tried for a crime that is never specified. He is on trial simply for being himself. But what is his great sin, what is he doing wrong merely by existing? Somehow K feels vaguely guilty simply by being accused, and yet he cannot identify what he is guilty of. The answer is not given anywhere in the text, and yet it is manifested in the very text itself. His crime is certainly not the pursuit of any ambition resulting from pride, and therefore not one of which he is aware, for there is only modesty and hesitance in his manner and, at all times, deference to authority. This surely mirrors Adam's humility at all times before God. Rather, K has absolute respect for the logical reasoning ranged against him by officialdom: he just doesn't understand the endless delays and alterations to his case. Indeed, he does not even understand the case against him at all; but what comes across is that he does not anyway feel *entitled* to understand the law, but merely accepts that he has to conform to it as best he can:

> Progress had always been made, but the nature of the progress could never be divulged. The lawyer was always working away at the first plea, but it had never reached a conclusion, which at the next visit turned out to be an advantage, since the last few days would have been very inauspicious for handing it in, a fact which no one could have foreseen. If K, as sometimes happened, wearied out by the lawyer's volubility, remarked that, even taking into account all the difficulties, the case seemed to be getting on very slowly, he was met with the retort that the case was not getting on slowly at all, although they would have been much further on by now had K come to the lawyer in time. Unfortunately he had neglected to do so and this omission was likely to keep him at a disadvantage.
>
> Franz Kafka, *The Trial*

It is evident throughout that the only way K ever tries to solve any of his problems is by asking questions, i.e. by incessant conceptual thought (avoiding at all costs contradictions). This seems innocent enough, and yet it sows the seeds of his guilt. The more complex the obstacles to establishing the nature of the charges against him, the more carefully and patiently he attempts to think his way around them – implying that this is the only form that knowledge or understanding can take. He is thereby making what I have previously called: the Cartesian Assumption. Thus K is not guilty of intemperance or anger or any other overflowing of passion, still less of pride; his fault is one of feeling too little emotion rather than too much. Instead he is trapped in a legalistic world of logical thoughts, constantly pairing various concepts with various objects, in a labyrinthine world of rules and regulations of never-ending complexity. This is a world governed by logic: to every thought there is a complementary negative thought – with which it cannot coexist and, to avoid a contradiction, only one must be chosen. But it is nevertheless a world with which K is complicit; at no time does he try to break the system, for like both the fallen Adam and Descartes, his own besetting sin is his inability to comprehend anything that is not a precise and consistent thought.

It becomes clear that the reason K simply accepts the legal system arrayed against him is because *it is his own mind*. In reality, for each of us, no legal system is imposed upon the totality of our mental processes from outside; we can only do it to ourselves. Thus K himself is deeply implicated in banishing his own transcendence. He at no time tries to step outside or transcend the system of law but at all times conforms to its seemingly interminable complexity, thereby increasing his complicity with it. Thus we see that the outer imposition of a trial is really an allegory for his own inner endorsement of there being no knowledge or action other than thinking and willing, respectively. In this way we may identify the nature of K's crime: he has, in effect, committed murder; he has murdered his own soul. The legalistic thinker the world has made him become has forced him to sacrifice his humanity; and perhaps the implication is that he was even like this before he was ever brought to trial.

His crime is that he never loses faith in the patient execution of methodical thought, and it is this unbroken production line of thoughts itself which denies the possibility of any alternative to thought such as intuitions, or self-awareness: for there is nowhere such an alternative could dwell. Indeed, it seems to declare that he, K, is nothing but thought; and for this belief he has been arrested. *The Trial* is an indictment against modern man: it is in the ceaselessness of the sentences and the lack of mental gaps that Kafka ultimately expresses the crime of K. It surely comes as no surprise when K finally accepts his inevitable death sentence with equanimity. Was the penalty justified? By living without faith, K had sleepwalked through life; he had merely existed without really living, and that had in any case been a form of living death.

And yet ironically, the result is undoubtedly a work of literature, and so despite it all, Kafka's parable does invoke faith in transcendence, but not the faith of the hapless K himself, rather the faith of the reader, whose enjoyment consists, as in all art, of transcending the ideas expressed in the text. The appreciative reader is not herself sleepwalking, but is enjoying a literary work – something K, with all his legal preoccupations, is unlikely to have had time for. As also with Beckett's 'Unnameable', Kafka could not help conveying to the reader, by the use of a metaphor, a faith which he apparently believed was not justified; and he did so by means of a *mode of understanding other than thought*, which his own book implies is impossible. And so it seems to me that he subverted by his own artistry the negative message he was trying to convey: he expressed by the quality of his own writing a faith for which he honestly saw no rational foundation. And that itself is Faith.

Chapter 11

Overview

What have we accomplished? We have seen how enlightenment provides a higher judgement which can be used to solve problems; consequently, we may identify it not only as knowing who you are, but also as a higher form of intelligence. I have analysed this as our miraculous ability to reinterpret symbols, enabling us to say man is not merely a user of previously inter-preted symbols, i.e. a thinker, but also a *creator of new meanings* with which to think. This must inevitably be a mystical experience, not describable by our previous meanings. And, while this has been a theory about the *concept* of enlightenment, we have seen that grasping enlightenment is not at all the same as grasping this concept.

Given that Enlightenment itself is inconceivable, each of the major religions has been led to symbolize it indirectly via various myths and allegories. The chart (Fig. 3) documents the widely recognized process of psychological transformation or change of life, either towards one of controlling will and desire, or towards transcendence of that will. Each column in Fig. 3 represents a different myth or parable in the various religions; however, the truth or falsity of these stories is not relevant to our current interest, for even where these (such as the Exodus) may claim a measure of literal truth, my aim is to compare them rather in terms of what they symbolize. In each case the first column lists a metaphorical image for the existential choice itself, the second column lists images for the predominant use of the will, and the third images for the pre-eminence of transcendence in one's life.

Now the question I should like to raise is this: in what I have written here, given that enlightenment cannot be conceptually defined, have I said anything different than these various allegories; indeed do my words about reinterpreting symbols other than by conceptual thought themselves then constitute nothing more than just another mythology? Surely not, and for the following reason. In most (but not all) of what I have said, I have not needed to resort to metaphor, but I have been able to speak literally. Likewise, some of what is symbolized by most myths could also nowadays be said literally (with concepts sufficiently advanced), and it is only part of the myth that can only be said symbolically and in no other way. This is the merit I should like to claim for the modern philosophical analysis I have developed here: viz, not that it succeeds in avoiding symbolism and thereby defines the indefinable, but that in my account only what *has* to be said symbolically, the indefinable, is said symbolically, and everything else is said literally.

A Comparison of Some Religious Myths

	EDEN	*EXODUS*	*AFTERLIFE*	*TIGER SUTRA*
CONTRADICTION	Temptation	Wandering In Desert	Limbo	Hanging From Vine
THOUGHT	The Fall	Bondage In Egypt	Hell	Two Tigers
TRANSCENDENCE	Paradise	The Promised Land	Heaven	Taste of Strawberry

Let us then compare, in each case, the images in Fig. 3 with the analyses of them previously given here. For example, in the first row is depicted the confusion or conflict of life's choices, especially the existential choice itself, in which we allow ourself to make decisions that are unclear: we are deciding whether to eat from the tree, we are 'wandering in the desert', in a state of limbo, or dangling on the vine of indecision. This is a suspending of the will, an experience of conflict or contradiction; but can we not surely express it as literally just that, without the need of these various images? Similarly, in the second row the images of The Fall, bondage in Egypt, two tigers may all be adequately replaced by saying the mind has decided to engage in the hard work of determining *all* its actions purely by the will, i.e. only by choices clearly conceived in thought.

However, I submit that these abstract interpretations were not available at the time to the authors of these myths; the ancient religions lacked our modern analytical tools. For the discipline of logical thought they had to refer allegorically to bondage in Egypt, or being threatened by tigers. And for the indecision of contradictions, they vividly described wandering in a desert, or hanging from a vine, as they were clearly unable to describe these things by the logical abstractions themselves. But we, however, are able to refer to these aspects of their myths without the use of metaphor, because we do now possess the necessary logical and psychological vocabulary.

But the final phase, given by the third row, is not so easily replaced by abstract psychological vocabulary: in order to explain that, it has been necessary for me also to use a kind of 'myth' in the form of a joke or a poem to communicate the capacity of the mind to transcend concepts. For that was the whole point about transcendence: that it is not possible to literally define it by means of thoughts, *no matter how abstract*. One might, for instance, think about transcendence without ever having experienced it: in such a case one would not fully understand it. But since everyone has experienced light-hearted humour and paradox, I satisfy myself that, by building on these, I have also successfully conveyed the more serious understanding of transcendence for life in general; but only by resorting to the communicative power of a modern equivalent of myth.

Thus, while bondage in Egypt can nowadays be expressed by the abstraction 'Thought', construed with its logical ramifications, the relief given by the 'Promised Land' must nevertheless remain a symbol (for the understanding of paradox) as we have no literal word or concept for it. Why is this? Understanding the concept of a bird or a skyscraper is the same as understanding birds or skyscrapers themselves, ditto for 'thought', 'confusion', *but not* for 'transcendence'; for understanding the concept of transcendence is not enough for us to understand transcendence itself. This is because transcendence is not understood merely as a concept having instances, but is a different kind of understanding altogether; we grasp it only when we grasp it not as the reference of some concept, but non-conceptually, as *a response we make to our concepts*. It is grasped as a mental skill. We, however, see that 'bondage' was inexpressible not due to this, but only because the biblical authors may have lacked the psychological concept of disciplined thought, i.e. the ascription of concepts to objects, disciplined by logic.

The first two rows thus contain concepts which the biblical authors could well have had, but just did not happen to possess in their civilization at that time. However, the 'Promised Land' was inexpressible for a quite different reason, for it refers to an experience that it is impossible to express in *any* language whatsoever, past, present or future – because it is the transcendence of language itself. And it is because this transcendence is experienced as complementary to conceptual thought that conceptual thought can never be used to define it. For this reason, we may concede that even the modern abstract terms *Enlightenment* or *transcendence* can only be understood symbolically, for no literal definition of them can ever be given.

However, granted that, for this reason, my theory is not fully expressed, and does indeed partly rely upon our understanding some of its sentences in a symbolic or 'mythic' manner, then I nevertheless believe this mythic character of my own narrative to be of a very distinctive kind in two different ways. Firstly, it is a narrative in which the maximum that can be said literally is indeed said literally, and only what can in its very nature not be said literally is said symbolically. Thus, in my account, I believe that what is said symbolically is kept to the bare minimum of what can be said in no other way. This is not the case for religious allegories such as the Exodus, or the two tigers.

Secondly, even though at a crucial point I have relied on symbolic exemplars, these exemplars have not been prose narratives like a myth, but have been poems and aphorisms taking the form of contradictions. A myth by contrast is normally intended to be, if not literally true, at least self-consistent, whereas the symbolic exemplars I have cited, like Zen koans, have been deliberately self-contradictory. They have nevertheless, however, been intended with similarly universal significance. I have done this in order to portray Man as a creator of meanings, able to transcend such contradictions in general. In this way, I have attempted to combine the concepts symbolized by religion with those used in logic and cognitive science by suggesting an irreducible mystical component to human cognition. This is the thesis that our normal everyday exercise of concept-formation must only ever be experienced as mystical, insofar as it cannot be fully defined by means of whatever concepts we currently possess, and so cannot be understood by us in terms of them. Indeed, I went so far as to say that all our aha moments of finding new meaning, such as humour, poetry and art, can be regarded as mystical simply in virtue of the novelty of the understanding they create and require.

One may perhaps sum up the philosophical approach I have adopted by saying that the rigorous methods and tools of Western analytic philosophy have been applied to the problem of the modern human condition as portrayed by Continental

European philosophy. It is this which has enabled us to endorse in analytical terms a cognitive solution to the problem, having its ancient roots in Eastern philosophy. In the process, our familiar concept of rationality may be said to have been modified, for we have seen that it may not only be rational to pursue logic in our reasoning, but at crucial points to instead pursue illogic, in full awareness that one is doing so. For it is only the illogic of self-contradiction that can invoke intuitions leading to conceptual change. In this way, I believe it has been shown to be desirable to incorporate an element of the mystical into practical decision-making, as a matter of routine. For contradictions can have the practical value of leading us to entirely new concepts, not available to the hypothetico-deductive method, which could not have been conceived otherwise. Indeed, it is the very mark of any new concept that it contradicts existing concepts explaining the same subject matter, otherwise it could be expressed logically in terms of them, and so would not be new.

In a variant of dialectic it was indicated, by means of concrete examples, how by using only *parts* of a conflicting thesis and antithesis we may combine some of these parts – despite contradiction of the wholes in which they are contained. As a result, the contradiction may in these cases be reinterpreted ambiguously as a bivocal pair of voices whose dialectic now enables a middle way between them to be found, in the form of a synthesis. In this way, we have combined a Socratic view of dialectic with the Middle Way of Buddhism. At the same time, it would appear that in so doing, we were eroding the schism between Eastern and Western thought which began with Descartes.

On this analysis, enlightenment provides us with a new view of rationality, a new approach to human reason, in which unreason is sometimes seen to be valued, but of course only at the requisite moment, the aha moment. In this way, enlightenment can lead to wisdom in one's affairs, by guiding us away from always endeavouring to be logical, towards first querying whether perhaps we may have the wrong basic concepts, and then seeking by intuition the meaning-change that can result from contradictions. One such mechanism for doing this has been identified here as the splitting, during an aha moment, of a single inconsistent concept into a pair of new mutually exclusive concepts.

Transforming your life

How does such a cognitive account of enlightenment compare with Buddhism itself? Zen in particular presents riddles to undermine logical thinking, but lacking a general theory of concepts tends to hint rather than explain how these bring peace, relieving us of conflicting desires. Buddhism, however, also has a different end in view: like all religions, it provides instructions to help you change your life, whereas I have confined myself so far to a purely philosophical description of life, using concepts encouraging the reader to think thoughts concerning the limits of these very concepts. Philosophy of course comprises only thoughts, and I have required the reader to think thoughts about concepts and also thoughts about thoughts. Especially, I have presented thoughts about the benefits of an understanding beyond thoughts, while at the same time emphasizing that these particular thoughts do not in any way replace that understanding.

Such a philosophical quest has not necessarily been intended in itself to induce enlightenment, but rather to do something secondary, viz: explain it, to the extent that it can be explained, like explaining a joke. And, like explaining a joke, this is something inferior to the joke itself. Paradoxically, I have hoped by these thoughts to also endorse the primary objective of encouraging people to seek and attain enlightenment by transcending such thought. And perhaps, for those already at peace with life, to understand better the nature of what they have attained, so as to apply it and communicate it to others.

The task I have set myself therefore has been primarily to explain and analyse, for the benefit of rational thought, how and when illogicality can in principle not only be rational but life-changing. However, unlike the religions, I have not seen it as my responsibility to recommend how to bring about the enactment of such enlightenment in one's own life. This, I have hinted, is an emotional change, unlikely to be accomplished merely by philosophical argument, however convincing. I have nevertheless demonstrated the pronounced advantages of enlightenment by various examples in which emotional and political problems have been solved (Chapters 6, 7, 8) when conflicting thoughts were transcended.

Perhaps the time has arrived though for me to at least attempt to indicate what pragmatic steps may be taken to develop an ongoing state of enlightenment, in order to improve one's life. For, having read my account, some may find that mere words do not suffice, and wonder – how can I actually *experience* enlightenment, how do I neutralize my own will so as to become a better person? Clearly this cannot itself be achieved by effort of will for, as so many have found, the will, in the very attempt to stifle it, merely expresses itself in a different form. Thus each such attempt merely perpetuates the very error it was intended to correct. My reply, in common with most of the religions, is that changing the habits of a lifetime may not be so easy, but that there are a few preliminary steps one can take.

We have noted, with Kafka, that the Fall of Man (the wrong existential choice) may not have been due to pride, since it can happen to the meekest of individuals. In other words, Original Sin may not be any of the normal sins or vices, or even any ill will, but it is nevertheless a matter of will in a larger sense. It is rather the manner in which the will is used; it is the fact that, regardless of any specific intent or purpose, there is a will to act in general only in pursuit of *intents and purposes*, to the exclusion of other forms of action. And it is this generality of will that we have to break; it is the universality of our controlling will that is the sin, not any particular act of will itself, for it is only the former that expresses our existential choice.

This is easier said than done; for we now realize it must also mean surrendering, as the basis of *all* our actions, the primacy of conceptual thought, the ascription of concepts to objects. Every thought is itself an act of will, and it is conversely thoughts which facilitate every desire and every intention, since we cannot desire what we cannot conceive. In demoting the will, we need therefore to find a way of acting other than by conceiving changes we want to make to ourself or to particular situations in the world. In other words, we even have to practise giving up, amongst other things, the thing we desire the most, namely the very concept of self-improvement and fulfilment. We need therefore to somehow find ways of committing ourself to such a new mode of life, by a means other than the will. This then is the seemingly impossible key to making the right existential choice: committing ourself, in the midst of active life, to suspending precise thought and will when appropriate and indeed to recognizing those occasions *when* it is appropriate to suspend thought. For the required life-skill is to know in practice exactly how and when to surrender thought, together with the commitment to do so in those cases.

To this end, the great religions of the world have all provided a specialized scenario, places of worship, in which to perform spiritual practices such as meditation and prayer, chanting and various rituals. It seems that the indirect purpose of these practices has been to temporarily replace logical thinking by behaviour that is deliberately non-logical. In this way, they mean to challenge the power of the logical, and introduce the possibility of an alternative. However, all too often, spiritual practices in a place of worship may not be mirrored in daily life, where self-interest is the norm. Yet the requirements of transcendence must affect all areas of life, not just religious ritual.

For a secular spirituality, we have seen that ordinary everyday actions can also have an aspect that is non-logical; namely, our ever-present preparedness to spiritually transcend whatever options are given by seeking new alternatives. This in itself may be regarded as a spiritual practice, but of a secular kind. Therefore, an important practical step I can recommend towards a more spiritually fulfilling life, apart from religion, is to find a special area of life in which you can value your own higher judgement of alternatives, allowing you – in other words – to always place transcendence before thought. What finer and more challenging scenario for this can we select than whatever it is we do for a living, our professional occupation? If we can perfect our conduct at work, then perhaps we might be able to extend this to the whole of life. With respect to this, however, there appear to be three major obstacles to implementing transcendence in the working environment.

Proficiency at work

Firstly, the absolute priority of transcendence requires you to be doing what to some extent comes naturally, and preferably to love what you do (q.v. Chapter 2). But if, in some occupation, you find you need to discipline yourself to proceed only by logical thought, then you are really only going through the motions of the task, not truly putting your higher self into the work; on the contrary, by self-control you are putting thought before transcendence. This may be exposed by the fact that when you hit a contradiction you tend to have no solution, no middle way, since you see the problem only in the same disciplined logical terms in which it was presented. For example, you may, for a particular problem, understand only the thoughts imposed by a fixed methodology, but not the limits of that method ('the limits of thought') and what may be beyond them. As a result contradictions, instead of posing intriguing challenges to your intuition, may produce a mental block for you in this particular field, as you plainly lack the necessary judgement to reconceptualize them. In such a situation, transcendence is not a real option for you, as you do not understand the material deeply enough to feel confident in going beyond the rules. This is a job for which (despite possible psychometric tests to the contrary) you feel no natural aptitude, since you are unable to apply intuition; such a job is bound to be stressful and may lead to failure and humiliation.

The preferable alternative is a profession that matches your real gifts, for in this case problems (contradictions) can often be transcended by your intuition and solved. Additionally, your colleagues will value the benefits to the shared enterprise of your private intuition, and respect your judgement, thereby enhancing your self-esteem. Admittedly, a humbler occupation may perhaps not utilize all the professional qualifications for which you had been trained, but it is also possible those qualifications examined mainly your ability to apply a particular methodology, and not your ability to judge the value or relevance of that method in any given case. Without the latter freedom of judgement, we have seen that it is hard for you to love your work, or produce work of real value to others. By contrast, a simpler occupation providing this freedom may, like Tolstoy's Levin mowing the grass, bring real fulfilment. This is because, while helping others, it may at the same time function as a medium of self-expression since, like Levin, you may find you are able to succeed at it in an effortless way, simply by being yourself. This is the ideal kind of work and surely, in itself, may be viewed as *a secular kind of spiritual practice*. However, unlike the Zen swordsman, in paid employment such self-expression is a bonus and is evidently not permitted to be more important than the intended result of the work. Nevertheless, if the required results are in fact generated routinely by acting naturally in this relaxed and contemplative manner, then one may perhaps say that such work counts for you as a spiritual activity.

If by contrast you are ineffective at the disciplined demands of your current occupation, or feel anxious about them, it may be because you lack the necessary flexibility and discretion exhibited by those with intuition for that type of work. Unlike them, it may be unclear to you when and when not to apply the rules and methods or, indeed, how to proceed at all when the rules or methods break down. In this case, you probably should accept that the activity was not meant for you, as you could not perform it in the relaxed manner with which you may perform other tasks that are more in tune with your real gifts. At least you have preserved your spiritual identity and have not become an automaton; for to lose your sense of self is a far greater failure.

Meaninglessness can also be a risk, when the work is so repetitive or dull as to provide no outlet for intuition or self-expression. In this case, you may feel alienated by the mindless routine of, say, a factory production line, or by the sheer futility of endless paperwork or pointless procedures that prevent you displaying any initiative. Thus with boredom, as with the previous case of failure, loving your work now becomes difficult or impossible.

Stress at work

As well as possessing the right mental resources to function effectively at work, you also need the right material resources. For there is a second major challenge to success at work, namely stress. In this case the work may be well within your abilities, but you may experience anxiety quite independent of your skills, due to the stressful demands of the job. In order to do any job you must be provided with the material resources with which to perform it. If, as is so often the case, to varying degrees, you are required to produce results with inadequate equipment, manpower or budget – or the results have to be provided within an unreasonable timescale – then this will induce feelings of stress in anybody, no matter how efficient or competent they may be. For not only are you being asked to do the impossible, but you are being held accountable for the results. This is the unenviable position of having the responsibility but not the control, and it breeds an air of unreality or doom, with the feeling that no matter what you do it will make no difference, you will inevitably fail. It is easy psychologically, but not logically, to move from this to the feeling that the fault is yours, that you should somehow be able to succeed with even deficient materials, and if you can't then it is you who are inadequate, not the job. In other words, stress can breed that state upon which we have been focusing so much in this book: a sense that there is a mismatch between you and the world, that no matter how hard you try you will fail; in short, *alienation*, a distancing between who you are and where you are going. Clearly, in the cause of self-preservation, this job also should be sacrificed.

Conscience at work

Quite apart, however, from these issues of professional incompetence, boredom or stress, there is another major obstacle to transcendence in the workplace; this concerns matters of moral conscience. Let us assume your intuition does have an opportunity for expression, and has no difficulty readjusting to the contradictions (problems) encountered within the confines of a particular job or role in an organization. As long as you are happy with the terms of your employment, it is indeed possible for you to love your work, transcending the contradictions that arise. In practice, therefore, you may feel spiritually free much of the time at work, because, not only do you sincerely believe in the value or importance of what you do, but you are given the necessary resources to do it and your decisions happen to be consistent with company policy. However, as part of a team, you do serve only the objectives set by company policy and higher management, and so there is always one conceptual thought you can never transcend, and that is your job description, as set forth in your contract of employment. Consequently, our job satisfaction can be seriously compromised if a situation arises in which we feel ourself to be morally in conflict with our job description itself; as an employee your duties may conflict with your wider conscience as a human being.

For example, you may be a company or government spokesman, compelled to make statements or speeches with which you strongly disagree. Or again, consider an attorney appointed by a court to defend a client she believes or even knows to be guilty. Officially, justice is the responsibility of the court as a whole, requiring each functionary: judge, jury, attorneys... to play its part. But justice itself is not this social system; it is an ideal which in any particular case may well not be rendered by the system. The attorney may thus be torn between her allegiance to the judicial system, and her allegiance to justice itself; a contradiction which the court may not allow her to transcend by abstaining. In accepting that the system should prevail over her own judgement she may not actually be doing wrong, but by helping a guilty man to evade prison it may instead be her own spiritual self that she is imprisoning.

More generally, an employer can easily give orders or impose procedures or principles of working which you are not free to transcend but must conform to, even though you may feel they are unfair or uncaring to the customer or the wider public. This is because the vested interests of a particular social or commercial organization may not conform to our own higher sense of social justice. While not actually breaking the law, you may even feel you are being paid to manipulate people unscrupulously, or exploit their weaknesses. For instance, by withholding vital information from them you may be required to mislead people into acting unknowingly against their own best interests, or against nature. Possible examples are: drilling for oil without concern for the environment or wildlife, planning roads or shopping malls without properly consulting people liable to be affected, and thereby disrupting local communities; or selling insurance without mentioning hidden conditions. In such cases, while not actually illegal, your job may be requiring you to do wrong; for while appearing to assist people in one way, your role may actually have the effect of harming their greater interests in another way. For example, a particular design methodology may well produce desirable low-cost housing, but at the undisclosed price of producing an ugly built environment, susceptible to vandalism.

Clearly your job description requires you to act only in the interests of your employer, and not on behalf of any of your other concerns. Nevertheless, you as an individual remain morally and spiritually responsible for the wider effects of your own actions, even as an employee of someone else, because *you choose to be that employee*. In cases of conflict, the prerequisite to preserve your spirituality is of course for you to transcend both your duty to your employer and your knowledge of the other social consequences of your work, so as to find a middle way between them. But this, your contract of employment, being uncompromising, will not in general permit you to do. In clear cases of malpractice you can become a 'whistle-blower' and, with difficulty, perhaps retain your job. But in subtler cases of beneficial employment with certain harmful side effects, such as a salesman being instructed to not mention serious disadvantages to his product, or the example given earlier of being ordered to teach a deaf child to read by methods which alienate her (Chapter 2), there may be no alternative but to resign your post.

The case of the Job Description is a very clear example of life situations in which, as a result of not being permitted to prioritize transcendence over conceptual thought, we may feel forced to act in an unenlightened manner, i.e. contrary to our existential choice in life. In these particular cases, we experience a contradiction between our social knowledge and our job description and we are not permitted by the job to transcend that contradiction. This may be why so many middle class professionals feel such a sense of malaise: it is because, however idealistic and compassionate a profession may aspire to be, it is always a social organization seeking vested interests and defined within a fixed conceptual framework. Hence by definition, it can never fully accommodate the essence of humanity – which is to make new concepts, since it is already defined by one particular set of concepts. It is for this reason that it is always an error to equate your life with some particular career; there can be no such career as spiritual freedom.

The fact is that often in our careers we embrace the social rewards of professional esteem, high remuneration and influence, in return for signing a contract of employment. If we do suffer conflict with our professional obligations, our commitment to the transcendence of thought provides a clear choice: it always requires us to first preserve the essence of our humanity, over our apparent duty. The solution, both for our happiness and our peace of mind, may be to modify or change our occupation in order to feel we can be more spiritually free.

This may, in any case, be a key to spiritual fulfilment in general. For, although one's initial illumination may have come swiftly in a Zen-like manner, the improvement in one's life is not likely to arrive with the same abruptness, but is rather a reward for one's increasing commitment. Consequently, as many of the religions have found, it is liable to take place only gradually, perhaps after many years of spiritual practice. If this spiritual practice takes the secular form of a change of occupation, the altered perspective of your new commitment may change your priorities progressively, leading you to treat people differently and vice versa. In this way, changing to work that you love, and experiencing your own ability to create meaning in what you do, can be the first faltering step to finding out who you really are, and where you are going in life.

Notes

Chapter 1

1. Inspired by a similar cartoon of unknown origin.
2. William James, *The Varieties of Religious Experience*
3. Jean-Paul Sartre, *Existentialism is a Humanism* (1946)

Chapter 2

1. FC Happold, *Mysticism: A Study and an Anthology*

Chapter 5

1. Many cognitive scientists believe that understanding a joke might be defined via some complex computational procedures in the brain, of which we are unaware. But if so, then there is nothing in principle to prevent us later *becoming aware* of these procedures and if they define humour we would be able to discern the humour by consciously following them. Yet this must be a fallacy because we can never be compelled to laugh at a joke purely by following a procedure. Indeed, telling the joke is itself a procedure, and then the laughter is up to us.
2. Logicians might say the meaning of the joke can only even be described (but not defined) in a single language, if it is a metalanguage referring to the two object-languages of the joke narrative, but cannot be adequately described in any single object language. However, the actual meaning of the joke, while not being linguistic at all, is nevertheless generated only by the two object-languages (i.e. the joke narrative), and does not itself require the use of any metalanguage.

Chapter 6

1. To assert that *friend* = *friend* means the two occurrences of *friend* are coextensive; in other words, that the first occurrence

of *friend* is true of an object if and only if the second occurrence is also true of that object. This too is a principle of logical discourse.

2. Contraries can, however, both be *false* of an object at the same time. E.g. Gil may be neither a close nor a casual friend of a person, since she may be something in between – or she may of course not be a friend at all.

Chapter 7

1. Philip Martin, *Shakespeare's Sonnets: Self, Love and Art*

Chapter 9

1. Nagarjuna, *The Fundamental Wisdom of the Middle Way*, trans JL Garfield, Oxford 1995
2. Similarly, Christian spiritual concepts such as faith are not feelings, but are nevertheless experienced as inexpressible. Perhaps these too may benefit from similar treatment, e.g. No-Faith etc.
3. DT Suzuki, *Zen Koan as a Means of Attaining Enlightenment*

Chapter 10

1. If we view the rejection of life as a spiritual state of Error, then this mechanism may have some relevance to the riddle of Nagarjuna (Chapter 9) concerning how such a state of Error might develop from individual actions.
2. In the Muslim Quran there is no such sequence, since here the serpent tempts both Adam and Eve together, and not, as in the Bible, just Eve separately, who then tempts Adam. The latter appears to base a cognitive transition, common to both men and women, upon sexuality.

BOOKS

Iff Books is interested in ideas and reasoning. It publishes material on science, philosophy and law. Iff Books aims to work with authors and titles that augment our understanding of the human condition, society and civilisation, and the world or universe in which we live.